D1435684

My Dolce Vita

Other books by this author:

Villa d'Este Cookbook

Villa d'Este Style

Tales of Risotto

My Dolce Vita

A Memoir Jean Govoni Salvadore

Foreword by Pamela Fiori

Glitterati
INCORPORATED

For Luca

First published in 2011 by

Glitterati Incorporated
225 Central Park West, Suite 305
New York, New York 10024

www.GlitteratiIncorporated.com
Telephone: 212 362 9119
media@glitteratiincorporated.com for inquiries

First edition, 2011
Library of Congress Cataloging-in-Publication data is
available from the publisher.

ISBN: 0-9823799-2-7
ISBN 13: 978-0-9823799-2-9

Copyeditor: Kristen Schilo
Design: Sarah Morgan Karp/smk-design.com

Printed and bound in China.

10 9 8 7 6 5 4 3 2 1

Contents

Preface

Rita Levi-Montalcini, an Italian scientist of neurology, is the oldest living Nobel laureate and the first to reach a one hundredth birthday. Levi-Montalcini was awarded the 1986 Nobel Prize in Physiology or Medicine, along with her colleague Stanley Cohen, for their discovery of nerve growth factor (NGF).

When I read the interviews she gave on her birthday, I was impressed by her remarks. Levi-Montalcini explained that she had been active all her life and that is what kept her young. She found that she had fun writing her autobiography, *In Praise of Imperfection: My Life and Work*, and had many happy recollections.

Thanks to Rita I thought, why not try my luck and take the same approach? It would be a means of keeping my mind alert—and besides, it was fun digging up my past! Irving Hoffman had put the idea of a memoir in my mind so many years ago; but reading about Rita Levi-Montalcini doing it at the late age of 79 inspired me to actually sit down and start writing my own.

So here I am at the tender age of more than 84 putting together my memories. I was born in Paris during the roaring 1920s when, according to Ernest Hemingway, the city was a "moveable feast;" I lived in Rome through World War II under the Fascist regime, the German occupation, the bombardments, the partisan uprising, and the liberation of Rome; I was involved in the beginning of the exportation of Hollywood via TWA to Italy, which led to La Dolce Vita; and, last but not least, I have spent the last forty-two years at the grand hotel Villa d'Este on Lake Como, named the best hotel in the world in 2009 by *Forbes*.

I have quite a story to tell.

Jean Govoni Salvadore
Villa d'Este, Lake Como, Italy

Foreword
Queen Giovanna

The title of this memoir may have drawn its inspiration by a film by Federico Fellini but its author bears no resemblance to any of its jaded characters. However, if the Italian directors Roberto Rossellini and Vittorio de Sica had known Giovanna Govoni Salvadore, they would have surely cast her in one of their movies or even built an entire script around her. Rossellini might have chosen her instead of Anna Magnani as a central figure in his 1945 neo-realistic *Roma, città aperta (Open City),* which echoed Giovanna's own World War II and post-War experiences. De Sica could have added her to one of his light-hearted comedies such as *Ieri, oggi, domani (Yesterday, Today and Tomorrow)*—as a foil for Sophia Loren. (Imagine the banter between them.)

Giovanna—who is also known as Jean—is that kind of woman: imposing, charismatic, full of mischief, loquacious, and brimming with anecdotes about the famous people she has encountered in her eventful lifetime. And, yes, she knew them all—except for one, but I won't give that away. I'll let her tell you herself.

Giovanna's particular story is a rich, multilayered one, starting in Paris where she was born to highly educated Italian parents on May 16, 1926—a Taurean to her core. Her father, a prominent newspaper correspondent, took his family with him wherever he was posted—mostly London or Paris—which enabled Giovanna and her younger twin brothers to learn proper English and French and be exposed to those cultures at an early age. With nanny Bertha and family dogs (one was named Chang Kai-shek), they lived a sophisticated life.

The Govonis were recalled to Italy in 1939 when war broke out, where Giovanna began for the first time to learn Italian. For years, the family had been moving between Paris and London—until the beginning of World War II--and there in Rome the real drama begins.

With her flaming red hair and freckles, Giovanna was not your typical Italian teenager. Indeed, she looked more like a poster child for Ireland. Her striking appearance made her stand out in the crowd and she was thus noticed by the Allied troops and became a Red Cross volunteer when the war was over and the American troops entered the city.

That chapter of her life is merely the beginning of a series of episodes all leading to where she is now lives and works: at the great hotel Villa d'Este on Lake Como. Giovanna herself is a legend to all who have known her—and there are legions of us. I met her and her beloved husband Luca on a sunny Sunday in New York almost forty years ago. I was introduced by Giovanna's longtime friend Karen Kriendler Nelson, whose family co-owned the patrician "21 Club." But that's not where we got together. Rather we convened at the far more plebian P.J. Clarke's on Third Avenue and had—I remember it to this day—Eggs Benedict and Bloody Marys. We got on famously and promised to reunite—which we did countless times through the years, sometimes at Villa d'Este, sometimes in New York, and once in Houston.

With Giovanna, you don't just get her; you also inherit those who are most precious in her life. I've gotten to know her children, Claudia and Andrea, now grown up with their own kids. Through Giovanna, I've become acquainted with Jean-Marc Droulers, the elegant *capo* of Villa d'Este, and with Annamaria Duvia, who has worked by Giovanna's side and is her "go-between" when it comes to sending and receiving e-mails. All of us, her admirers, sit at her feet and listen intently (many times over) to her tales, urging her to put them in writing. Her excuses: Too busy. Too distracted. Not up to it. Who'd want to read them anyway? Finally, Marta Hallett, her editor and publisher, took her by the shoulders, sat her down and said, "Now write." And write she did.

It is said that everyone has a compelling life story to tell. But some, like Giovanna Salvadore's, are simply more compelling than others.

Pamela Fiori
New York City

Introduction

I will soon be celebrating my birthday, and before I leave this troubled world, I want to put together a few reminiscences, which I have registered in my diaries. From childhood, keeping a diary has helped me organize my life. As Mae West said a long time ago, "Keep a diary, hon, and one day it will keep you!" I was taught to keep a diary when I went to school in England, and today I have a wooden chest containing more than seventy diaries, which I have enjoyed reading over the years, time permitting.

Some fifty years ago, when I was working as public relations for TWA in Rome, I had a wonderful friend, Irving Hoffman, a top press agent both in Manhattan and on the international scene; he had made a name for himself as a columnist for the *Hollywood Reporter.* He was a buddy to Truman Capote, Pablo Picasso, J. Edgar Hoover, the Maharani of Baroda, Elizabeth Taylor, Marilyn Monroe, and countless VIPS to whom he wrote hundreds of letters a week. And he also wrote to me. I have a chest that holds dozens of his letters. How I ever rated to become his friend I don't know! I was certainly fortunate in this and also because he repeatedly encouraged me to write my autobiography.

Unfortunately Irving died in 1968, and without him I was lost and gave up on writing. It took me another forty years to take his advice, and to write this book.

I started my compilation some years ago by recalling the war years, but it became quite obvious that I would have to dig a lot more into my past. I have such a vivid recollection of my early years, the cities: Paris, London, Lugano, Rome, Milan, where I lived with my family until I moved to Villa d'Este with my husband, Luca, in 1967. This is where I am right now.

The war years certainly left a mark on me. At first, life at that time was almost like a Hollywood production of a war movie: There were the "bad" guys and the "good" ones, but as time went by, it became so that you couldn't tell who was right and who was wrong. Of course, the fact that food was becoming scarce and there seemed to be German snipers behind every street corner turned life into worse than a movie, something more like a nightmare.

But this was as far as I would get, the war years. I continued to try to expand beyond this time, but I would draw a blank; I would pause for a couple of days; and then start all over again.

Finally one day I was chatting with some Villa d'Este hotel guests on the terrace overlooking Lake Como. Because I consider Veronica and Stuart Timperley good friends, having known them for ten years, I raised my concerns about the actual creation of a memoir. They quoted Mark Twain.

Finally in Florence in 1904, I hit upon the right way to do an autobiography, Twain wrote: Start it at no particular time in your life; wander at your free will all over your life; talk only about the thing which interests you for the moment; drop it the moment its interest threatens to pale, and turn your talk upon the new and more interesting thing that has intruded itself into your mind meantime…

This got me going. The handwritten words finally started flowing, and I began to really enjoy the memories and the process.

It is amazing how much I can recall by just skimming through the pages of my diaries. I kept reminiscing about the years (twenty in all) that I spent in public relations for TWA and consequently for Howard Hughes.

I have to confess, once and for all, that I never actually met Howard Hughes.

I liked to refer to him as my boss—which is the truth because he owned TWA (at least 78 percent of the shares) and I reported directly to him via his office and spoke frequently with Noah Dietrich, his right-hand man. I received requests to handle all the film stars and Hollywood gossip columnists traveling to Rome via TWA. And I had been instructed never to use his name and to ignore the usual name-droppers who would call to announce that they were buddies of Howard Hughes. When confronted with this type of "reference," I immediately answered, "Let me check the VIP list that was sent to me by the big boss!" They always backed down without uttering another word.

Then the movie *The Aviator,* based on Howard Hughes's life, came out and was distributed worldwide. It was a big hit, and Hughes became even better known around the world. So many people would ask me what was he like in person. Of course, I could not answer, and most of the time I would say, "You will read about Howard Hughes when my book comes out." One thing was made crystal clear to me when I worked for him: Howard Hughes didn't want to be mentioned in the papers, and I was told that "nothing would please him more than never to see his name in print." I feel I knew him because once, when his aunts, Mrs. Martha Houston and Mrs. Fred Lummis, arrived in Rome as tourists, I was advised to go all out for them. We spoke about their precious nephew, and he soon became our favorite topic of conversation.

Working in public relations has helped me come out of my shell. I was actually a very shy person until I was forced to be otherwise by my work.

How I came to work in the public relations field is easy to explain. . . I enjoy people and I can speak English!

It meant a lot when the war ended because the English language was sure to open doors for you. French was out, and English prevailed.

I had no idea what public relations was about, and I didn't go out looking for the job. It was offered to me because I came from a family of journalists and my English was surprisingly good for an Italian. So why not give me a chance? I certainly was very lucky, because this was the time when Rome became the capital of "movieland" and a visit to Hollywood on the Tiber was everybody's dream.

World War II ended in 1945, and I was already working at the American Red Cross, when I met my future husband, Luca. In 1949 we married. We were both twenty-three years old and in those days you didn't get married unless you wanted to have children. This was a great time for us. We took trips practically every weekend to attend an opening on Broadway or to visit a new restaurant in Paris, because we had a pass from TWA that enabled us to fly all over the world. As a wedding gift, we were "given" Giulia, a maid of all trades, who said that unless we produced a child, she would quit. I couldn't afford to lose her, so we promised that in nine months' time she would become a nursemaid.

My son, Andrea, arrived punctually, and I insisted upon nursing him between one VIP arrival and another. Racing around on my motorbike one day, with both children in tow, I nearly dropped them (daughter Claudia had arrived two years after Andrea). It was time to get a car, so we chose the cheapest that we could find, buying a Fiat 600 on the installment plan.

In the meantime, celebrities arrived and I tried to meet them all: Ingrid Bergman, Audrey Hepburn, Ava Gardner, Greta Garbo, Vivien Leigh, Joan Fontaine, Elizabeth Taylor, Greer Garson, Lana Turner, and many more. Robert Taylor arrived with one wife, Barbara Stanwyck, had an affair with an Italian starlet which precipitated a divorce, and left Rome with a second wife, Ursula Thiess. He was at that time considered the most handsome movie star since Rudolph Valentino.

I organized a couple of megaparties, including the One of 500, to celebrate the inaugural flight of Rome to New York. In 1962 I attended the inaugural of the TWA Flight Center at Kennedy Airport in New York designed by famed architect Eero Saarinen. Another memorable party was the 1966 TWA twentieth anniversary celebration. I continued to meet the most interesting people, many referred to as jet-setters: Gore Vidal and Tennessee Williams, and many others.

In the late 1950s, after Claudia was born, we moved to a larger apartment, which had a garden so we could keep a dog, much to my joy. In the meantime we had built a small villa in Fregene, the fashionable summer resort in the vicinity of Rome.

Luca had accepted his job with Rizzoli in Milan, and I began my stint (now some forty-two years in the making) at Villa d'Este. Shortly thereafter, he left Rizzoli to set up a sales office for the hotel, on the condition that he shave his beard, which I rather fancied. But I was anxious to have him with me, so he accepted, and we had a great time together. When the hotel closed for the season, Luca and I would travel to the States and all around Europe. He would contact the travel agents he had met during his TWA days, and I would look up the press. At that time it was all done by word of mouth, so many contacts have become friends. Forty, fifty years have gone by, and I am still in touch with many.

We created promotions and events to get people interested in our hotel. One idea was to start a cooking school and give classes to the local people from Como. We thought of giving classes for English-speaking pupils and, of course, Italians. This proved to be a great success; nearly forty years later, these classes are still in great demand. Word got out, and the cooking classes became not only the talk of the town, but word reached the United States, and we were invited to participate in the Philadelphia kitchen of Julie Dannenbaum where our chef, Luciano Parolari, did a great job. Julie Dannenbaum was one of the early chefs in America in the 1970s, who popularized gourmet cooking for the general home cook.

It became part of the Villa d'Este program to visit the U.S. on an annual basis for promotional purposes both in terms of the cooking school classes, special food-related events, and to boost public relations in general. Soon our kitchens at Villa d'Este were swarming with ladies, at first, and eventually, with gentlemen, all wanting to cook in the Villa d'Este style. During the 1970s anything to do with cooking was "in." We received many requests to give classes to groups who would have a meal after the classes to see if they enjoyed what Luciano had taught them. Clients such as Kidder, Peabody, Ideal Standard, and Pensions 2000 were eager to include a cooking lesson in their programs. In addition, hotel clientele changed as younger visitors began booking because Villa d'Este had so much to offer thanks to the many facilities available: eight tennis courts, full aquatic sports set-ups, and three swimming pools—one floating out on the lake.

One party that will go down in history took place June 26, 1973, to celebrate the 100th anniversary of Villa d'Este as a hotel. In 1975, I was invited to the White House for lunch. This was during the Gerald Ford administration, and the menu consisted of Villa d'Este signature dishes. Because the cooking students would ask me for the recipes, I started writing cookbooks. The first, *Cooking Ideas from Villa d'Este,* came out in 1981; the second, *The Villa d'Este Cookbook,* was published in 1999; and *Tales of Risotto* appeared in 2006. In between I also wrote *Villa d'Este Style* (2000).

Disaster seemed to be on my doorstep starting in 1986, beginning with the fact that my Luca had some serious health issues. He seemed to bounce back and even insisted upon making our usual U.S. trip. On returning to Villa d'Este, Luca's condition deteriorated, and January 22, 1988, he passed away. I was adopted by Luca's friends, and they helped make it easier for me to overcome my terrible grief. My children (today in their fifties) came to keep me company and to decide on my future. I insisted that they should return to their homes while I planned to brave it on my own.

In the summer, my pregnant daughter came to visit. I thought that summer on the island of Elba, where we owned a dreamy little house in Poggio, a village dear to Napoleon (who was exiled on Elba), would be a restful place for Claudia and myself. We didn't have time to settle in, though, because Claudia nearly lost her baby. We returned to Villa d'Este by ambulance. Luca, my grandson, named after my Luca, was born prematurely on September 26.

At the end of October my doctor discovered that I had cancer. What a year! But I recovered, and all seemed to finally be on an even keel.

I certainly take it for granted that I'm living in one of the most beautiful spots in the world, and I can understand that many of our guests suffer from withdrawal symptoms when they leave. I felt the same after visiting Australia for the first time in 1970. At that time the hotel wanted to expand horizons, and Australia seemed the next best country to conquer with the allure of the hotel. Always with the goal of expanding our culinary reach, I accompanied Luciano Parolari, our chef, to Australia, where he gave three weeks of cooking classes in Sydney and in Melbourne. Consequently, many Australians helped fill up rooms at the hotel.

In 1995, we really hit the jackpot when we received an invitation for Luciano to supervise the restaurant at the dining room of the United Nations for the month of April in order to celebrate the fiftieth anniversary of the U.N. Foundation. In November, Luciano was officially invited to prepare a dinner at the United Nations, in honor of Kofi Annan, soon to become the Under-Secretary-General for Peace Keeping Operations. Also in 1995 we discovered the latest trend: the "chef's table." At the U.N., this had become a vogue. On one of these occasions I met Julia

Child. We had a ball exchanging recipes, and she promised to visit with us—although we knew that she was definitely more inclined to order foie gras instead of spaghetti!

I found that I was spending more time in the States than I had expected. I guess it was due to the fact that my Claudia and Andrea were so well established in the U.S. that I thought I should join them, at least in the winter. So I started looking for a pied-à-terre. I was thinking of Greenwich Village, but my son talked me out of it: "What is an old lady like you going to do in the Village?" he asked.

Without taking offense I moved my search uptown, and with the help of friends I found what I needed: a large studio. This became my nest away from Villa d'Este, and I'm sure that my Luca would have approved.

Unfortunately once I got settled I had some health problems. Now I am all patched up and raring to go. Read about my life, and then come to visit me at Villa d'Este . . . or shall we meet in New York?

Ciao for now.

Part One
The War Years
1926-1946

I never met my paternal grandparents, who originally came from Bologna, but I heard a lot about Gastone Chiesi, my maternal grandfather. His family came from Modena. He was a staunch republican and, I'm told, the patriarchal type. A note of irony: A young Mussolini worked as a messenger boy for Grandpa, who was editor-in-chief of the daily Italian *Gazzetta del Popolo*, while my great-uncle was the managing editor.

My maternal grandmother, Emma Schlaefli Chiesi, was from Bern, Switzerland.

My great-grandfather ran a store selling musical instruments in Bern.

Nana, as I used to call her, had a very handsome profile, and she was chosen, at the age of seventeen, as the most beautiful girl in the country. Her image was to be sculpted on Swiss coins. When he was approached officially, her father was indignant: "Never! How dare you! My daughter will not jingle in every other man's pocket."

Nana was very dignified, and everybody called her Madame Chiesi.

My father, Giancarlo Govoni, was a correspondent for Italian daily newspapers, working from Paris and London.

My mother, Isabella "Isaly" Chiesi, was a "woman of letters," a librarian who loved to spend her free time at the famous bookstore Shakespeare and Co. in Paris—a meeting place for the intelligentsia of those days. Sylvia Beach owned the store, and all the literary world would pass the time of day there, including James Joyce—whose book *Ulysses* was published by Beach—Gertrude Stein, Alice B. Toklas, Anaïs Nin, F. Scott Fitzgerald, Henry James, Ernest Hemingway, and many more. The French writers were represented by André Gide, Paul Valéry, Jules Romain, and other distinguished authors of the day.

My parents were married in Milan in 1922 and first moved to Paris, where I was born on May 16, 1926. Three years later we moved to London, where my twin brothers, Mario and Italo, were born. My father

worked variously in London or Paris—depending on his assignments—
for some years to come as a foreign correspondent for Grandfather's
newspaper. He always wanted his family with him, because his work
meant he could write at home rather than in an office. Thus we traveled
back and forth with him and made our homes in Paris and London
over the years.

Before I go any further with the story of my life, I want to introduce
you to Chang Kai-Shek. He was my first doggie when I was four years old.

Dogs have always had an important role in my life. I am told that my
mother would have "Ole Faithful" (his name was Fido) watch over me
while I was in the cradle or the crib. In later years I trained the dog of
the moment to guard my kids when they napped in their prams in the
garden. (I believe it is most important to have our children learn to love
animals, chiefly dogs, by growing up with them.)

After Fido died, my parents immediately replaced him with a purebred Pekingese named Chang Kai-Shek. He had a great personality and
was very vain. I was a very little girl when I got him, and he was there
on my first day at school; he had his photo taken with me. I was dressed
in my uniform of the La Sagesse Convent in Golders Green, London.

That day, the two of us were also immortalized in a drawing, which
hangs in my bedroom to this day.

I remember asking my mother if we would get another doggie when
Chang Kai-shek passed away. Mother assured me that we would
definitely adopt another dog, but it could not be a Pekingese. She
explained that sometimes if you do not change the breed, because
you love your dogs so much, you end up looking like your beloved pet.
And my mother added, "Take a look at Countess Pecci." She lived in
our apartment building, and I often ran into her when she walked her
pets. She owned three or four Pekingese dogs. Well, you can imagine!
The first time I ran into the contessa after my little conversation with
Mother, I nearly burst out laughing in her face. Mother was right; the
countess really *did* look like her doggies.

Poor Chang Kai-shek, he was a victim of my kid twin brothers. One
day they stuck their lollipops in his mane, and we had to have him
shaved. The poor darling was so mortified that we had a coat made
for him to hide his embarrassment.

Time passed by, and when Chang Kai-shek closed his eyes forever on September 1, 1939, Hitler's troops crossed over to Gdansk, Poland, and the Second World War began.

During my early years in London, my first love was Dirk Bogarde— my childhood boyfriend who went on to become a renowned actor, writer, and painter. I met him when I was about six years old. I had just started school and was in the same class as Dirk's sister, Elizabeth; to this day she is still my very dear friend.

Dirk was a few years older than I was. After school, we spent a lot of time together because we lived close by and our parents were friends. Dirk's father, named Ulrich, was the art director of the *Times* of London, and I used to call him Uncle Bogie. Dirk's mother, Margaret, was on the stage before her marriage. She was my favorite, and I used to call her Auntie Maggie.

When we were children, Dirk confided in me and said that when he grew up he wanted to become an actor, a writer, and a painter, but he hadn't quite decided which of the three roles he preferred. I guess he never did decide, and this is why he later succeeded in all three of his aims.

In his first autobiography, *A Postillion Struck by Lightning*, he wrote:

> *I have said that we, as children, hardly ever made friends. This is not strictly true in the case of about four people, three of whom were at school with me, the other, a girl, who was Italian and lived with her Roman family not very far from us. Her name was Giovanna and she was my sister's best friend and they went to school together… I tolerated Giovanna Govoni because she was very, very nice and nearly like a boy. And although she was strictly speaking my sister's best friend, she was often at the house and kept out of my way so I was not disturbed. On the other hand she seemed to be interested in snails and frogs and stick-insects, and kept goldfish which brought her nearer to me than the fact that she spent hours with my sister looking at this absurd baby, which had crashed into our midst.*

There was another reason for my liking, even accepting, Giovanna as a friend. And that was her mother's cooking. When you went to their house, not unlike our own but a bit bigger with an old chestnut tree in the garden, it was not at all like going to anyone else's house I knew. Although the walls, and rooms, and even the furniture, conformed to the English style in every conceivable way, the atmosphere within those walls was more Roman than it was London. There was always a most delicious smell of cooking: of basil, of garlic, of rice, and of olive oil. The family, Uncle Gianni and Aunt Isaly, plus their twin sons, Italo and Mario, who were very much younger than we were, filled the house with music, laughter, screaming, and violent conversation which I found both stimulating and exciting.

In his third autobiography, *An Orderly Man,* written about the pre-war years, he mentioned my family again.

The Govonis had been recalled to Rome some time before, but Giovanna was sent back to stay with us for a holiday to "keep up her English." The telephone now rang almost constantly from Rome with worried appeals to get her back as soon as possible. My father and I drove Giovanna down to a boat to Newhaven and shoved her up the bursting gangway filled with anxious people carrying bags and suitcases. We waited on the quay until eventually a small, weeping redheaded figure fought her way to the stern, waving, sobbing and crying out, "I love you. I'll never forget you. Good-bye, good-bye." The sirens went, gulls screeched, and the packed ship moved gently away from us. She stood there waving and waving until the ship made a slow turn to port at the end of the long jetty and bore her away, out of my sight, for twenty-three years.

When it was published, Dirk sent me an autographed copy of the book, which was inscribed: "I love you too!"

In 1935 Mussolini attacked Ethiopia, and the League of Nations applied economic sanctions on Italy. This meant that father's pay check would no longer arrive in London, where we were living by that time, by regular mail; it might not arrive at all in England. So Mother decided that since Father's earnings were sitting in Italy, that was where we should be heading. Mother convinced my father that a change of scenery would do my brothers and me a world of good, and instead of spending a dreary, gray holiday huddling together at the Eastbourne seashore, we spent the summer basking in the scorching sun of the Lido of Venice.

It was my first visit to Italy and, although I had started to learn some Italian, it was decided that I should attend school in Switzerland. In the meantime, Mother and my brothers, who were not yet six years old, traveled from hotel to *pensioni* (as the funds dwindled), covering the whole Lake Maggiore region. By 1936 sanctions against Italy were lifted, and the Govoni family moved back to Paris.

At first I was sent to a very snobbish French school on Avenue Victor Hugo, where, despite the fact that I could hardly speak Italian, that I was fluent in French, and that my flaming red hair made me look like an English tomboy, I was immediately nicknamed *la petite macaroni.* This was the only unhappy period of my life, and although I tried to stick it out in my typical stubborn fashion, my parents soon became aware of my problem of not being accepted. I even developed a complex about speaking French because I was constantly ridiculed.

I was then enrolled in a brand-new Italian school that had just been inaugurated on Rue de la Faisanderie, a stone's throw from where we lived on Avenue Bugeaud. I felt quite at home in this model school because my chums' parents came from a social milieu similar to that of my parents; there was a large community of Italian expatriates in Paris in the 1930s.

The number one Italian daily, *Il Corriere della Sera,* did a story in December 2006 on home tutoring—fashionable in the days between the two World Wars. In this article, Bertha Dunz from Stuttgart, the Govonis' governess during one of our stints in Paris, was mentioned.

In our Paris household Bertha took over, and she insisted upon my learning to speak German. I was scared stiff of her, and I sure learned to master the language, which became useful to me during the German occupation of Rome. She was a mystery to us all, but she did a good job. She became a "jack of all trades" in our household, donning different headgear according to the occasion. Dirk Bogarde was sure she was a Nazi spy, and he wrote about her in his first biography, *A Postillion Struck by Lightning.*

In 1939 we left Paris for Rome (without Bertha), at the outbreak of the Second World War. The German troops had entered Gdansk and were to stay there permanently from that point on.

Upon returning to Rome from Paris, I automatically became a member of the Fascist Youth Organization. Not that I had any choice! The only way this could have been avoided was if my parents could have afforded private schooling for me in one of the plush and expensive convents run by nuns, which they could not.

On Saturdays, dressed in a white cotton shirt with a black cotton pleated skirt and a fez with a pom-pom, we marched up and down the streets of Rome. I soon became disenchanted with the Fascist regime and sought ways to get out of these Saturday afternoon rallies. I discovered that I could be excused if I joined the Giovani Italiane Cavalleggere (Young Italians on Horseback). I had to work hard to make the grade, but at least I didn't have to march up and down the streets of Rome anymore. Instead I would parade on a horse once a week, up and down the Via dell'Impero.

As a teenager, I thought only about doing well in school. I was attending the classical lyceum, which meant that I had to learn ancient Greek and Latin, while I was still having trouble learning to speak Italian.

I had to try and forget the English language entirely because, during Fascism, I would have been in trouble if anybody heard me speaking anything but Italian or German.

In August 1942, thanks to Bertha and her insistence on teaching me the language of Goethe, I was selected, along with eleven other girls from the major Italian cities, for my outstanding knowledge of German. As a prize, we were sent on a month's tour of Germany.

The trip was cut short because of heavy Allied bombing. My roommate was Ida Visconti di Modrone, a relation of the late movie director Luchino Visconti. Her educational background was similar to mine.

When on our own, we would lapse into English, and our fits of giggles were considered scandalous and unmilitary. We wore Fascist uniforms. Most of the trip was spent visiting the hospitals and entertaining both Italian and German soldiers by singing Fascist hymns! It was taken for granted that, being Italian, I would have a passable singing voice, but to everybody's amazement it was quickly discovered that I could not carry a tune. From then on I received orders to move my lips and not let out a sound.

The trip was a frightening experience because wherever we turned, the Gestapo was checking up on us. I vowed never to return to Germany, a promise that I have kept to this day.

Although Italy had entered the war in 1940, life in Rome was still bearable in 1942, apart from the air raid alarms. Food was rationed but no problem to secure if one could afford black market prices! Some items were becoming scarce: Clothing was purchased with coupons, and leather could be found only at exorbitant prices.

In 1942 the first air raid alarms caught Romans by surprise, but we followed the instructions and took shelter in the cellars of our houses and apartment buildings. At first we young ones thought it was a game, with alarms ringing night after night, and finally it was decided by the majority of people in our building that nothing that would threaten us was happening, so why not go back to bed? The reality was, of course, that if a bomb had dropped directly on our building, we would have all been buried.

The bombs were dropped at night, so our windows were covered with black sheets of paper to keep light from filtering out through the shutters. But on August 17, 1943, the Allies landed in Sicily, and at that time Rome was bombarded in broad daylight as a last-gasp effort of the Germans. The naïve Roman population stepped outside to watch the planes flying overhead, the bombs were released, and thousands were killed.

Having attended a half-dozen schools in four different countries—France, England, Switzerland, and Italy—I finally settled down in the Visconti High School of Rome in 1940. Originally built in 1522, Visconti was one of the best-known public schools in Italy. Pope Pius XII completed his studies here, as did many other famous people.

I immediately made some friends, and I have managed to remain in contact with them to this day. The school was noted for being a den of anti-Fascists. The most representative one was our art professor, Raffaele Persichetti. He was so handsome, tall with dark curly hair and blue eyes; he looked as though he had stepped out of *The Thorn Birds*, the novel by the Australian writer Colleen McCullough. All the female students were madly in love with him, including me.

Once during his class he was trying to explain the famous Venetian painter Titian when, all of a sudden, he spotted me. He came over to my side, caressed my hair, and solemnly announced, "This is the *color* I was looking for: Tiziano. From now on I will call you Tiziana."

I was in a sort of trance—and to think that I had wanted to dye my hair! Unfortunately this budding romance ended before it ever started. It ended on September 10, 1943—the day the Nazi-Fascist occupation of Rome started and which lasted until June 4, 1944. On that day, several students, led by Raffaele Persichetti, and some civilians in shirtsleeves improvised barricades at Porta San Paolo to obstruct the advance of the German tanks. They all died . . . but not in vain. This tragedy inspired the Romans to fight the occupation and create the Resistance, which was instrumental in opening up the road to the Allied forces.

Paolo Salimei, a school chum of mine, was a very sweet and kind boy, especially toward me. I had to put up with a lot of teasing, and he always stood up for me. I was still in the throes of learning Italian (and was also studying ancient Greek and Latin), and with my knowledge of English and French, I was easily confused. This became a laughing matter among my classmates whenever I made a mistake in pronouncing a new Italian word.

Paolo didn't live far from me, and we often walked to school together. One morning, without warning, I heard a shot, and Paolo fell to the ground in a pool of blood. It all happened so suddenly that I had no idea how it happened, but since we seemed to be alone on the street, I can only assume it was a German sniper. I became utterly hysterical. Some people, I guess they were Italians, shoved me into a doorway until I calmed down. Paolo's death was a horrifying event, but many people witnessed these terrible things during the war years.

Later in 1943 life became more and more unbearable. I am somewhat surprised, when I look back on it, that so many of us survived. For example, on October 16, the Fascists rounded up 1,022 Jews from the Roman ghetto. They were sent to the Auschwitz death camp, and when the war ended, only fourteen women and one man were returned. Of course Father, who had made it back from exile on the Italian and Austrian border, lost his job. For a while we lived on our father's collection of gold coins.

The Allies landed in Anzio, the beach near Rome, January 22, 1944. In a matter of hours they could have reached Rome because the Germans were ready to leave, but to this day nobody knows why the Allies got stuck in the foxholes. My father, in the meantime, just up to this time when the Allies arrived, had been exiled, like many other journalists and writers who were not in harmony with the Fascists. I don't remember what my father said or wrote, but we were happy to have him back in Rome.

The horrors of war reached a peak on March 24, 1944, with the Fosse Ardeatine massacre, when the Germans executed hundreds of Italians in "reprisal" for an Italian Resistance attack the day before.

The atrocity and its aftermath have been described profusely, most notably in Robert Katz's book, *Death in Rome*. However, the massacre is still relatively unknown, and, not widely discussed by the people who lived through it, probably because it was such a horrendous event.

The reason why I remember the exact date is because I happened to be in the center of Rome, close to Via Rasella, that day, when a column of German policemen was attacked by partisans. A bomb, hidden in a rubbish cart, was pushed into position by a partisan disguised as a street cleaner, and shortly thereafter it exploded, killing thirty-three German soldiers. I was out with my mother at the time of the blast, and we quickly took refuge in a store until we were sure that the Germans had moved on.

When Adolf Hitler heard of the event, he ordered a reprisal: For every German who was killed, for every German death, ten Italians were to be shot as compensation. First the Italian prisons were emptied of inmates for the slaughter, but there were not enough victims to reach the quota of three hundred and thirty.

This is when the Fascists, together with the Nazis, chose men at random from the street. As we lived near the blast, our neighbors started disappearing. The cobbler who repaired our shoes and lived in a cellar on my street was picked up without an explanation, and we never saw him again. Many other inhabitants of Via Rasella were added to the list. It is said that even the Germans were horrified by the orders, which came directly from Hitler.

The victims were taken to the Ardeatine Caves outside of Rome, and the killing squad, consisting of German officers, went to work. The victims, in groups of five, were made to kneel down and were shot with their arms tied behind their backs. Next another group climbed on top of those who had just been killed. This went on all day until three hundred and thirty-five victims, stacked one atop the other, were killed and then sealed into the caves. After Rome was liberated, on June 4, 1944, the caves were opened, and the victims were given proper burials.

It was a terrifying experience. We were informed later that no women were included in the many roundups, but we had reason to worry for our men. Soon after the war, film director Roberto Rossellini made a movie titled *Roma, città aperta (Rome, Open City),* which depicted the atrocity, starring the Italian actress Anna Magnani. Hollywood was forever changed by the advent of this film, which initiated a new era of realism.

During the war years, when we were down to the last coin, we looked around to see what we could sell, but we were out of luck because all our friends were in the same boat as us. Accidentally, I put my horseback-riding ability to use.

My dear friend Sofia Berti lived next door, and we shared a friend. Her name was Carla del Poggio, and she was an actress. The movie director Mario Mattoli was filming a movie about girls in a posh sort of finishing school. Title of the film: *Ore 9 Lezione di Chimica (Nine O'Clock Chemistry Lesson).* It was difficult to find girls who could ride horses, so I was often called upon, and I was happy to make a few extra lira.

When I went to see the movie, I realized to my surprise that for most of the film I was shot from the back! But it seemed not to matter: I soon became known as a stand-in stunt girl. Yes, I had to throw myself from the horse! That is probably when my aches and pains started . . . the ones that plague me to this day. I made another movie, as well, again appearing mostly from the back: *Corona di Ferro (Crown of Iron)* with actors Osvaldo Valenti and Luisa Ferida, who always acted together and were lovers as well. Later they were shot to death by the partisans because they were Fascists.

And I found another way of making money: giving English lessons to various high-ranking Fascists, who thought that it would be a nice gesture to greet the "liberators" in English. To me this meant that the majority of the Italians had already given up hoping to win the war! The first student, a certain General H. Ercole, contacted my father because my father was known as a journalist who spoke English. My father told people about the fact that I was giving lessons and before I knew it, just through word of mouth, I had put together a whole class of Fascist students who wanted to be prepared. (On the sly I got to know some partisans, and I gladly gave them English lessons for free.)

My third job was as a courier for the partisans. Initially my job was to memorize messages and deliver them to contacts living on Via Nizza. These messages were all delivered on foot, as the Germans had already requisitioned my bike. Walking Rome was pretty harrowing at the time, and I sometimes wondered whether we Italians would ever emerge from the wartime horrors.

In the course of giving English lessons and delivering messages, my first student, the general, fled to Portugal (the homeland of his wife) without paying for his lessons, and I never heard from him again. But I didn't care, because by the end of May it became common knowledge that the Allies would arrive soon. Knowing this, I had become very active and reckless in carrying arms back and forth to the partisans.

There also came a time during the German occupation that shoes could not be resoled—there was simply no leather. Since I was always running around delivering messages, I would do what everyone else was doing: I would cut cardboard into the shape of a half sole and tuck it inside the shoe when holes appeared. Sheets of newspaper were spread across the chest under threadbare coats. Overcoats and men's suits were turned inside out. Tablecloths and curtains were made into dresses. In the summer we all learned to make sandals out of rope and canvas. They were known as "Capri shoes." Today they are called espadrilles.

Regular meals became pure fantasy. Most people did not smoke nor drink—even wine was not available. Ingenuity was a means of survival.

There were several times in my life when I was overwhelmingly happy, but the liberation of Rome topped them all because it meant that, thanks to the Fifth Army, I was alive! For months the Romans, including me and my family, had been waiting for the Allies to come up from Anzio, where they had landed in January 1944.

Instead thousands and thousands of Allied soldiers lost their lives sitting it out and waiting for the big shots to make up their minds as to the "Liberator": General Bernard Law Montgomery (Eighth Army) or General Mark Clark (Fifth Army).

On June 4, 1944, a friend, Eugenio Galdieri, who lived south of Rome near the Porta San Paolo (I lived north of the city), called in the evening to announce that he was watching the Allies from his window. They were parked outside every front door on his street. Some soldiers were sprawled out and fast asleep; others were dozing propped up against the buildings. They were waiting for the last German to leave town. Later it was made known that a gentlemen's agreement between the Vatican and the German authorities, who occupied Rome, had been tacitly made: no bombing and no fighting in the streets of Rome. Rome, the Eternal City, had been declared an open city (inspiring the title of Rossellini's film masterpiece).

I shall never forget the dawn of June 5, 1944, when the city came alive. The whole population went wild with joy and was on hand to greet the liberators. This had to be the most unforgettable day in my eighty-plus years on this planet: the arrival of the Allied troops in Rome. With my family, I was living on a street parallel to the Via Flaminia, built by the Romans two thousand years ago, and the street on which the liberators entered Rome. Finally the nightmare of the war years was over, but it took nearly another year before the war in Europe ceased. Hitler, Germany, and the Nazis were never again acknowledged in Italy, and even in the schools there was no mention of Fascism

Six-year-old Giovanna Govoni (Jean Govoni Salvadore) with her dog, Chiang Kai-Shek, on her first day of school at La Sagesse Convent in London, 1932.

Firma del Titolare

Savoni Giovanna

Data del rilascio della Tessera

28 NOV. 1941
Anno XX

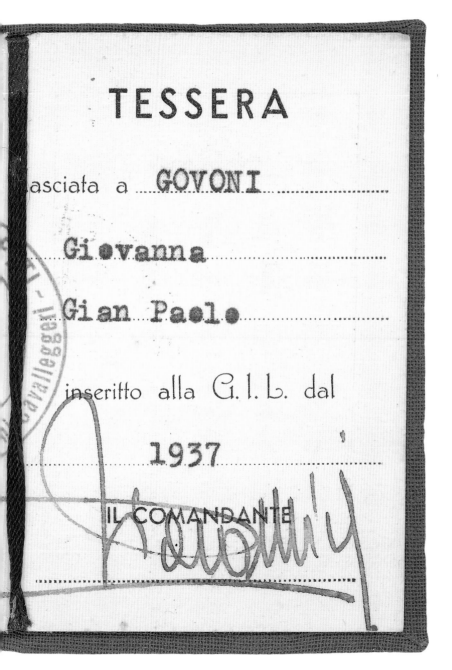

TESSERA

...asciata a ....GOVONI........................

........Giovanna................................

........Gian Paolo................................

...inscritto alla G. I. L. dal

...........1937...........................

IL COMANDANTE

Membership card for the horseback riding club the Giovani Italiane Cavalleggere (Young Italians on Horseback) of the Fascist Youth Organization.

Giovanna's mother Isabella "Isaly" Chiesi at 6-months-old.

Neighbors visit the Chiesi family (Isabella "Isaly" Chiesi, Giovanna's mother before she was married, is in the center) at their home in Croydon, London, 1915.

The author's maternal grandparents' (the Chiesis) home in Croydon, before World War II.

Right: The author's parents, Isaly and Giancarlo Govoni, in the 1950s.

Antonio Balconi
LUGANO

The author's grandmother, Emma Chiesi *left* and *right,* with her 18-month-old granddaughter, Giovanna.

Giovanna with her mother in Paris, 1927.

Giovanna's uncle, Gino Chiesi, a pilot during World War I.

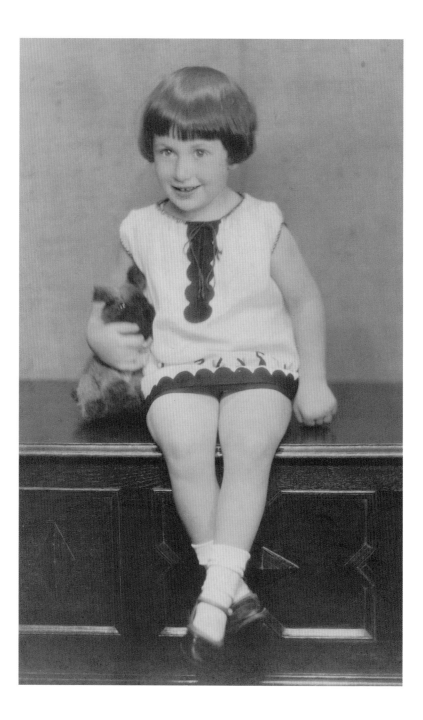

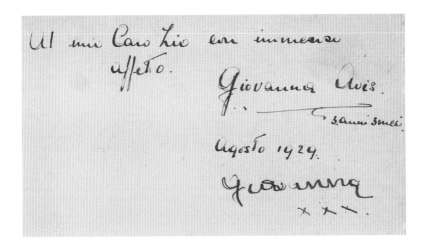

The author in 1929, at age 3, with a note that accompanied this photo when she sent it to her uncle.

To my dear uncle, with immense fondness.

Giovanna Avis
three years, three months

August 1929

Above: Giovanna with her mother and twin brothers, Mario and Italo, in 1936 and *right,* with her twin brothers on an excursion to Hastings, England.

Following: Bertha Dunz, the Govoni's German governess, with author Giovanna and twin brothers Mario and Italo in Eastbourne, England, 1934.

The author, far left, with the Bogarde family minus son Dirk, with baby Gary, mother Margaret, and best friend Elizabeth.

Right: Giovanna (holding the javelin), in training for the Olympics at her new school, the Visconti High School, once back in Rome in 1942.

Italienische Jugendfüh
wundete.

Auf Einladung der Reich
Jugendführerinnen eine
und finden überall bege
in der Reichshauptstadt
gross war die Freude de
Gesichtern der G.I.L.-Ma
schen Heimat- und Soldat
erkannten, den tapferen
geisterte Dankbarkeit de
schönster Lohn.

Aufnahme:Transocean/Schm

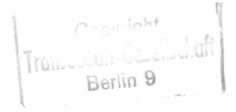

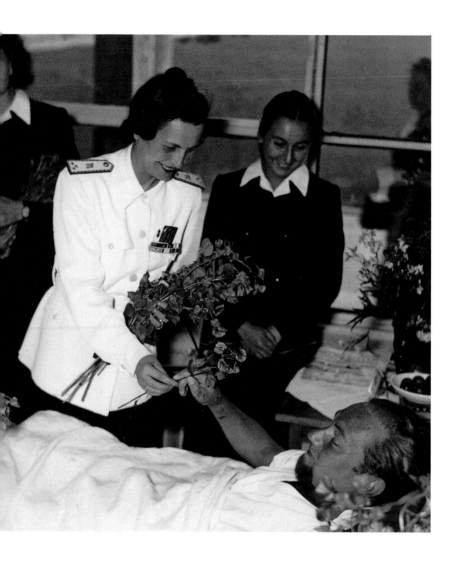

During World War II the Italian Youth, including the author, second from left, were invited by German Youth to visit the wounded, and were received most cordially. In Berlin they made the rounds of the hospitals, bringing flowers and singing patriotic songs to cheer up and comfort injured German soldiers who, in turn, expressed their gratitude.

ALLA CARA MEMORIA

DI

PAOLO DEI CONTI SALIMEI

15 OTTOBRE 1926   29 SETTEMBRE 1943

O Signore, che amabilmente ci avevi fatto prezioso dono del nostro Paolo, ora che egli ci ha preceduto nel mistero della tua gloria, concedi a noi di rivederlo un giorno nel gaudio dell'eterna luce.

Il 10 settembre 1943 cadeva eroicamente il

Professor Dottor

RAFFAELE PERSICHETTI

Tenente dei Granatieri

A tumulazione avvenuta ne danno straziati il triste annunzio i genitori: GIULIO e ALLIATA AMALIA; i fratelli: AUGUSTO, LUIGI, GEPPE, GIANNI; le sorelle: LUCIA KUMLIEN, MARIA ANTONIETTA STERBINI; gli zii e i cugini: PERSICHETTI, LOMBARDI e SABATUCCI.

Una preghiera per l'anima eletta

La presente valga come partecipazione personale.

Roma, Corso Rinascimento n. 101.

Left: Memorial card and newspaper notice of the death of Paolo Salimei, who was killed during World War II in Rome, 1943.

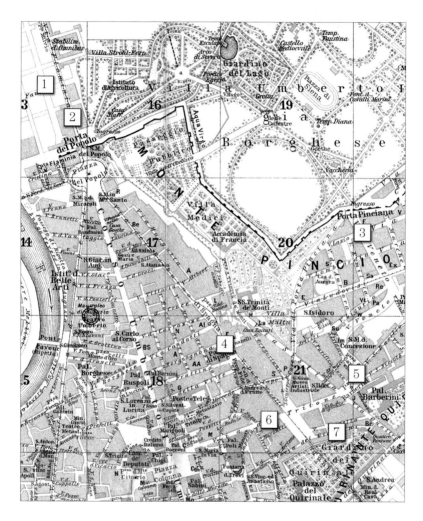

A 1909 map of Italy illustrates important locations in Jean's Rome. 1: Jean's family home on via Pisanelli; 2: The road to Florence taken by the escaping Germans followed by the 5th Army; 3: Via Venteo; 4: Piazza di Spagna; 5: American Red Cross where Jean worked; 6: Jean and her mother's shopping trip; 7: Site of the Partisan Ambush.

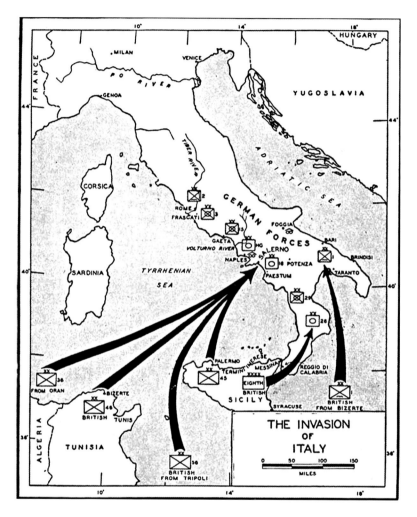

Map of wartime Italy shows the path of the American soliders who liberated Italy from Fascism on June 5, 1944.

Following: The entrance of General Clark and his troops is recorded in an important photograph.

TO: Miss Jean Govani

Jean:
Well you're not here either.
Shall try again one of these
days. I love you, Lyn

LYN C. WALTON
FIELD CORRESPONDENT

88TH DIVISION   5TH ARMY

Combat Correspondent Killed Near Montecatini

WITH THE 5TH ARMY, July 26 —The first 5th Army soldier-reporter casualty was disclosed today with the news that Pvt. Lyn C. Walton, 20, Arlington, Va., a member of a Division Public Relations Section, was killed in action near Montecatini on July 9.

Pvt. Walton was with an infantry company when the unit was subjected to heavy shell-fire by German artillery. Formerly classified as an advance scout, Pvt. Walton was appointed combat correspondent about four months ago. In civilian life he was sports editor of the Alexandria, Va., "Gazette." Prior to his last trip to the front, he had declined assignment to a rear area.

Notice of the death of Lt. Lyn C. Walton, war correspondent and "first love" of Giovanna on July 9, 1944 in Montecatini, Italy.

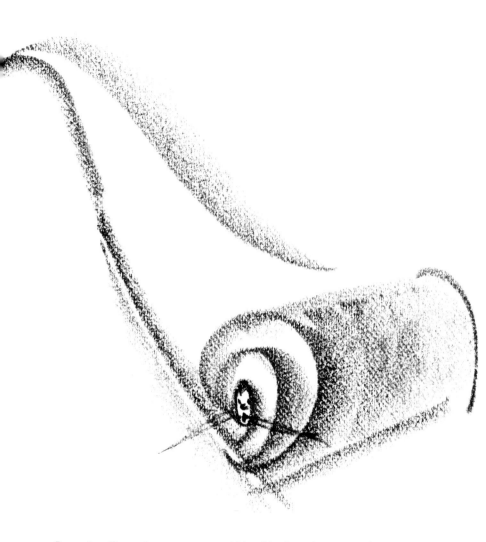

Preceding: The author, now renamed "Jean" by Stan Anderson, "Stan the Donut Man," third from left, poses in front of the American Red Cross Donut Canteen on June 5, 1944 as she is "recruited" by the US Army to distribute coffee and doughnuts to the troops as they enter Rome.

Above: Roll out the red carpet: Irving Hoffman, great friend and colleague of Jean as she moves into phase two of her life as the first public relations executive in Italy, creates a visual rendition of her career transition.

and the Second World War! In fact, the war became so invisible in Italy after it ended that it was necessary for my husband and I to fill in our children on this incredible omission.

The last of the German troops trudged along as they departed Rome, and much to our amazement, they were a bunch of kids. Certainly none were above sixteen years of age; none had even started to shave. It was a pathetic sight: Were these the "bad guys" who had kept us in awe for so many years? A silence fell upon us all as we watched the youngsters shuffle along, dragging their rifles. For the first time my heart went out to these poor children.

Finally, when they were out of sight, and after curfew, General Mark Clark and the Fifth Army made their official entry (just in time, because the Roman population was left without water and electricity. Everybody was out on the streets, cheering, hugging, and kissing.

This is when an American wearing an American Red Cross outfit stopped my mother and me. He had an armband: Stan the Donut Man. He overheard us speaking English (which we always did when Mother and I were together). Mother's hair was blond and my hair was a fiery red. We didn't look very Italian. We certainly did not resemble the typical Italian that Stan Anderson had in mind. Without wasting any time, he came right to the point: "I overheard you speaking English, and I need your help. I am requisitioning the building behind me"—that was the Banco dello Spirito Santo, the Bank of the Holy Ghost—"and I would like your daughter, I take it that she is your daughter, to get behind the counter and hand out coffee and doughnuts to the troops as they march on to Florence. By the way, what is her name?"

I said, "Giovanna!" and he replied, "Too difficult to pronounce."

I said, "And in English, it's Joan."

"Too limey!" said Stan. "We'll call you Jean!" It stuck, and to this day I am known to my American and British friends as Jean.

My mother said that of course I would volunteer because we owed it to the Allies that we were still alive.

On my first day of work at the American Red Cross canteen, I brought in a friend who lived nearby, but she didn't last very long. Her parents were titled, and it wasn't dignified for her to be seen by her friends in the neighborhood handing out coffee and donuts to the GIs. From then on I braved it alone, but instead of being paid, every evening I was given a bag full of doughnuts, on which my family dined.

Stan instructed me to keep the GIs queued up in an orderly manner as they waited in line to be served. I must admit they were very disciplined until one day about six soldiers came right up to the counter to get their coffee and share of doughnuts. I was indignant and ordered them to get in line.

"You heard her," some of the GIs chanted. "Get in line!"

At this point, Stan rushed over. "General, please excuse the girl; she is Italian and didn't recognize you."

This is when I found that I had been ordering General Mark Clark around. Stan couldn't fire me because I was a volunteer, and the general very graciously got in line and waited for his turn to come up.

The next day, word got around, and the three major news bureaus—International News, Associated Press, and United Press—showed up and wanted to photograph me because I was the first Roman girl to work for the American Red Cross. Shots were taken at the canteen on the Via Flaminia at St. Peter's Square and at the Coliseum. For a grand finale, they took a picture of me throwing donuts from Mussolini's balcony at Piazza Venezia. The story and photos appeared across the United States on June 10, 1944, exactly four years after Mussolini had made his declaration of war on France and England from that very balcony.

I remembered that when Mussolini had been making this historic speech, I had seen, amid the ocean of people below, one woman in particular who stood out in my mind. While Mussolini waited for the multitude's response with his hands on his hips and his chin jutting out in a typical pose, this woman grabbed her little boy, lifted him above her head with outstretched arms as if she was about to catapult the poor creature, and, seized by rapture, called out to Il Duce. Her loud voice boomed across the piazza: "Duce, so' tutti fiiji tua!"—"Leader, they are all your children!"

This meant that the women of Italy—obviously she was our self-appointed spokeswoman—were ready to sacrifice their children for Mussolini. At the time, I thought this affirmation was slightly exaggerated but sincerely touching. And as photographs were being taken of me on the same balcony, I wondered where that Roman woman was now. Her opinion must certainly have changed!

As my picture was being taken, Mussolini was still around—in Northern Italy, somewhere on Lake Garda—and this made me feel most uncomfortable. I felt utterly silly standing on the famous balcony where he had addressed the world by delivering his celebrated speeches . . . while I delivered doughnuts like a modern Marie Antoinette, substituting doughnuts for the infamous cakes. In the meantime, people were gathering below, wondering what was going on. What a grotesque situation! After all, Mussolini had revealed himself as a ridiculous character. Still, it didn't make sense. Nothing made sense anymore.

I was having trouble understanding the American way of speaking, and they made fun of my British accent, but I was beginning to realize that my liberators really were "crazy Yanks," as their English cousins often referred to them. I was concerned whether I was doing the right thing by going along with this entire extravaganza.

I should have asked my parents' permission for that photo to be taken, but little did I know where I would end up when I left the house that morning. I was probably not viewing this incident in its right perspective, and I had to be in the wrong or else something was lacking in my education. It was all very confusing! I had such mixed feelings regarding my "liberation."

Of course, I was grateful that the Allies had put an end to our misery by breaking the German siege of Rome, so why couldn't I make a little effort to be polite and stop worrying?

"Jeanie, snap out of it!" my photographer shouted once again. "Imagine, tomorrow you'll be a celebrity! Your photo will be in every paper from coast to coast!" I didn't really find this heartening news. My heart sank.

Who cares, I thought quickly, I don't know anybody in America! Aloud: "Oh, really!" in my clipped British accent. This set off another ripple of laughter.

That night the photo shoot was the main topic of conversation at the dinner table, as the family faced another plate of doughnuts. My father would explain to me the erratic behavior of the U.S. press corps.

Although the German soldiers had left, I did have a run-in of sorts after their departure. One day at the Red Cross canteen, a GI walked in with a most handsome police dog. I immediately decided that I was going to become a friend to it, so I put my hand out to caress the dog, but it was on the defensive and made a beeline for my nose. The owner managed to hold the animal back because he had it on a very short leash, so it only bit off half of my nose. I was immediately rushed to the American hospital, where my nose was put together with some Scotch tape and I was told that if it did not heal with this "bandage," then I would undergo some plastic surgery.

Jack Pierce was the dog's commander, and he was so embarrassed and upset that I invited him for dinner at my parents' home. There Jack explained that the dog had belonged to the German SS and was trained to go after prisoners who were trying to escape.

At this point Jack decided to ask my father for my hand in marriage. The answer was, "No way! You are a nice fellow—I don't think you deserve that scatterbrain of my daughter as your wife." To this day I have a scar to remind me of my foolish escapade.

I consider myself very lucky because I managed to live through the war years. Until the Rome liberation, we Roman natives really had a miserable time, and we never believed we'd make it. The last few days before the Fifth Army arrived in Rome, we were without water, bread, and the essentials of life.

But I am a survivor, and together with my family, I was catapulted into a completely new world. Fabulous times awaited me. I received more marriage proposals, and I think it was because of my red hair and freckles—they reminded the boys of the "girl next door." Of course, the fact that I spoke English helped.

I got to know the dirty, weary GIs. I met Bill Mauldin, the famous cartoonist who received the army's Legion of Merit for his contributions to soldier morale, when he came through Rome. I still have a copy of his best-selling book, *Up Front,* which won the Pulitzer Prize in 1945.

The day after Rome was liberated, I had met a fellow who introduced himself as Private Lyn C. Walton, field correspondent attached to the Eighty-Eighth Division, Fifth Army. I think I fell in love with him. He was a real nice guy, a true American lad who reminded me of an actor, not that we could see any U.S. movies (they were not available until after the war).

Lyn would come in to see me each day, and he would wait for me until I gave out the last doughnut.

My parents had told me to invite Lyn for a family supper, so it became a habit for me to take him home with me, and before I knew it my father had given his consent to our getting married once the war was over. My father had grown fond of Lyn because he was a reporter and they would have long chats about politics.

Then there was a long silence until one day as I was reading the U.S. Army newspaper, *Stars and Stripes,* I came across a news item.

Combat Correspondent Killed Near Montecatini
With the Fifth Army, July 26—The first Fifth Army soldier-reporter casualty was disclosed today with the news that Pvt. Lyn C. Walton, 20, Arlington, Virginia, a member of a division Public Relations Section, was killed in action near Montecatini on July 9th.

Pvt. Walton was with an infantry company when the unit was subjected to heavy shellfire by Germany artillery. Formerly classified as an advance scout, Pvt. Walton was appointed combat correspondent about four months ago. In civilian life, he was a sports editor of the Alexandria, Virginia, Gazette. Prior to his last trip to the front, he had declined assignment to a rear area.

I must admit that I really went to pieces. I was utterly heartbroken! My parents were most understanding. I was only eighteen years old, and I thought I would never be able to fall in love again.

For a long time I mourned Lyn Walton. Unfortunately I did not even have his photo . . . it was like waking up after a bad dream. I was still in my teens and I had my whole life in front of me—still, I wasn't eager to meet any boys and least of all to date anybody. I was perfectly happy to be on my own.

In the morning I would go to school—I was finishing high school—and from two p.m. to ten p.m. I would be working in the game room of the American Red Cross, which had now moved to Palazzo Ruspoli, located in the center of Rome. The building, which belonged to the Ruspoli princess, was quite breathtaking, especially for the poor GIs who had spent months lying in foxholes. Come February 16, 1945, I was wrapping packages and there was a long line of GIs carrying their war souvenirs, which I was about to wrap up. I found myself staring into the face of the most good-looking guy. Later I found out his buddies referred to him as the Golden Boy. He was tall, he was blond; but unfortunately I cannot remember the color of his eyes!

How to go about it? Should I send an e-mail to ask, after more than sixty years, "Excuse me, what color eyes do you have?" "Roberto," as I playfully call him now, seemed to me at that time to be the love of my life. I am sure he would be rather hurt that I can't remember the color of his eyes!

To make a long story short, Roberto reenlisted to remain in the army for another year. Only when he called his parents to tell them that he had met this Italian girl and had signed up to stay in Italy for another year did his father and mother threaten to cut their financial help, which he needed to finish college. With this new information in hand, Roberto decided instead to opt for an honorable discharge and went home about a year after we had met. I was distraught, and this time I was through with men.

I got my revenge, but that is another story.

This was the third time that I had been ditched. The first, dear Lyn, God bless him, was probably the most sincere, while Bill Livingood left me with a puppy and wrote me twenty-one letters, one a day—because that is how long it took his ship to cross the Atlantic. (More about this story in Part Three.)

Oh, well, all is well that ends well! However it took me a while to get over Roberto's departure. Obviously his parents were terrified by the fact that he was planning to bring home some "furriner" he had met who knows where!

Now I understand how embarrassed my Roberto was, when one evening he showed up at the American Red Cross to announce that he was going to take me to the opera, since he was leaving the next day for the States. I couldn't believe that this was the guy I thought I was going to marry. Instead he was walking out on me.

According to Roberto, it was an utterly romantic gesture to end our relationship with an evening at the opera! I boo-hooed through the whole performance until Roberto removed me from the audience. A year passed before I received a letter from him. He announced that he was about to marry a girl named Jean. He also admitted that he missed me! But that was all.

Years later I told my husband Luca about my romance, and because he was curious he looked Roberto up when he happened to be in Chicago. Later, I did the same, and Roberto took me around to meet his family. When I was introduced to his mother, I startled Roberto by speaking to her in my clipped British accent as opposed to my more American-style English. That was my revenge! We still keep in touch by e-mail. How romantic!

After my job at the Red Cross canteen, I was hired at the American Red Cross Club at the Casina delle Rose in the Borghese Gardens. Here my boss was Sally Steinman, who decided that I should be promoted to the wrapping department and the information desk. Now that I was on the Red Cross payroll, I was entitled to one meal a day.

I shall never forget what it was like to eat regularly and to know that I could look forward to a plate of chili con carne three times a week. The menu for the other three days was Spam. I was off on the seventh day.

I tasted Spam for the first time when Rome was liberated, just after my first day behind the counter of the American Red Cross canteen, passing out the coffee and doughnuts to the GIs. At lunchtime I was asked to follow the American Red Cross staff, and we went to the mess hall, where each one of us was given a tin of Spam. I thought it was the most delicious dish I had ever tasted. Those last days waiting for the Allies to come into Rome, I found out what it was like to go hungry.

Two days before the arrival of the Americans, along with a group of totally famished friends, I had assaulted an oven near the Ponte Milvio, which had been requisitioned by the Germans. Naturally it was off limits to the Roman population. Even our coupons were of no use, and if we got too close we were putting our lives at risk, because the Germans who were guarding the bakery would not hesitate to shoot us. We scrambled for safety, taking a few loaves with us.

All of this explains why I thought that Spam was a godsend and that from that time on, I decided to always keep a tin of Spam in the house: It was a symbolic gesture meaning that, as long as I had some Spam, I would never go hungry. So far it has worked and saved us from the life without water, bread, or electricity.

At the American Red Cross, which had its headquarters in the Bernini Bristol, one of the top Roman hotels, life was very pleasant. The building was new, the heating worked, and the décor was modern and comfortable. The GIs returning from the front lines on a three-day leave would welcome a few hours of rest in the spacious armchairs, where only a few months before German troops had lolled during the occupation period.

On one of these occasions I was working at the wrapping counter and a soldier came up to me carrying a big cardboard box under his arm. "'Scuse me, ma'am," he said, "could you hold this for me while I take a nap?"

"Sure," I replied, "I just came on duty and will be here until ten o'clock tonight."

The soldier then leaned over the counter and whispered: "I think I'd better tell you, there's a duck in there."

"Of course, soldier, do you want me to wrap him up?" I inquired.

"But I don't think you understand. The duck is alive and his name is Ben. He is kind of special."

"Okay," I replied, "so what am I supposed to do?"

"Ben," the soldier continued, "is our mascot, he fought right along with us and waddled his way up from Cassino where we first found him. I brought him to Rome today because my buddies and I decided that Ben should get a discharge and we want him to retire in a nice family atmosphere"—and without pausing he just went on—"would you like to have him?"

I sort of spluttered something unintelligible, but it must not have been effective since the duck was handed over to me with a flourishing "Thank you."

Before I had time to recover and explain that I lived in an apartment on the top floor without a terrace or even a balcony, it was too late because my friend had gone, leaving me with the box sitting on my desk.

I was utterly speechless and dumbfounded by the rapidity of the transaction until I suddenly heard a distinct quack resound from the cardboard box. I realized this was no joke.

Oh, well, I thought, I'll get rid of it. I guess I'll take Ben home tonight just for fun and then tomorrow I'll dispose of him somehow.

But as I had started to refer to the animal by his name it was already too late. I had unconsciously accepted him. Now how would the other members of the family feel about Benny? I knew my brothers would be delighted to have a pet; my father would not mind as long as I kept Ben out of his study; but maybe mother would resent having a duck in the house. I might convince her if I explained that Ben was a sort of hero and certainly the only duck to have fought in a war. There had been write-ups about Ben in *Stars and Stripes:* How Ben had saved some soldiers' lives by warning them with a quack of the enemy approach (similar to the *oche del Campidoglio* as in the history of Rome). Surely mother would not be able to resist to such a wonderful human-interest story!

That same evening I introduced Ben to the family, and he was unanimously accepted as part of the household. The only objections came from the maid, Maria, but since we were used to her disgruntled disposition, nobody paid much attention.

As the days went by, Ben got to know us all. He immediately recognized our footsteps as we walked up the main staircase and would salute us with a quack. He kept to his box a lot and would quack whenever he wanted to get in or out. Otherwise Ben was no bother.

Christmas approached and we were confronted with the problem of the traditional preparations bypassed during the war years. Maria was in charge of the Christmas dinner, and she promised to come up with something festive while I handled the decorations. We soon realized that Benny was central to her plans—she intended to substitute him for the Christmas turkey! Happily this was discovered before Ben fell prey to her plot, and instead we consumed a lovely Christmas dinner of Spam in the shape of a turkey.

And finally, the war ended in Italy in a very tragic way.

After the Allies secured Rome and Florence, the Italian army was dismantled because the Italian king, Vittorio Emanuele III, had abandoned the country. There was nobody left in charge. Everyone was obliged to look out for himself.

This is when we very nearly started a civil war. The Germans were fighting the partisans, whose numbers were increasing by the day, and the Italian soldiers were caught in the middle of it all.

Meanwhile Benito Mussolini, who was responsible for dragging us into this war in the first place, was trying to escape Italy. Who came to his aid? None other than Hitler himself, who gave orders that, upon Mussolini's arrival in Como, he was to be hidden in a truck filled with German soldiers. He was given a German army greatcoat and a helmet.

The truck just about made it to Dongo, on the Swiss border, but the partisans were waiting for Il Duce. He was brought back to Mezzegra (near Tremezzo on Lake Como), and eventually he was executed right above the lake, along with his mistress Claretta Petacci. Their bodies were brought to Milan and strung up in Piazzale Loreto for all to see. And so the war ended in Italy. It was the 1945. On April 30, 1945, Hitler committed suicide; just three days later, V-E Day marked the end of the war in Europe.

Part Two
The TWA Years
1946-1966

In 1946 I was still working at the American Red Cross at the Hotel Bernini in Rome, wrapping packages and giving directions to the nearest mess hall. Then one day I heard that the airline TWA was opening an office on Via Barberini, a few steps away from the Hotel Bernini. I inquired about employment opportunities and was told that ground hostess candidates were being interviewed.

I applied for a job and was accepted. I soon found out that my job consisted of meeting passengers upon arrival, walking them to the terminal, and putting them on a bus to Rome, then walking the departing passengers to the same plane for their flight out. Utterly boring! I was just on the verge of quitting when the TWA pilots went on strike—the day before Christmas so I was to stay home. I was relieved when the airline called telling me not to worry, I would be rehired. I was thankful because I missed working.

After that, my job became more interesting. In fact, the next twenty years with TWA were to be the most exciting in my life, and it was through my work there that I traveled and I met people from all over the world. During these years, I made so many lifelong friends—friends who I still visit, talk to, or think of every day.

Consider Caresse Crosby, an eccentric lady whose first acknowledged achievement was receiving the patent for the invention of the brassiere in 1914! She was also well known in the world of fine arts, with friends such as Beverly Pepper, Giò Pomodoro, and many others, from the years in the 1960s and 1970s when she lived in Rome. She was also a book publisher of some renown: Her company, Black Sun Press, issued books by Ernest Hemingway, James Joyce, and T.S. Eliot, among others. She died in Rome in early 1970, aged 78.

Caresse was a world traveler and suggested that I join her in her plan to "decitizenize" herself, by throwing out my passport and becoming a citizen of the world. I told her I would think about it. Fortunately my husband, Luca, stepped in and stopped me from taking any foolish steps.

My generation, meaning those of us who were born between the two world wars and who are still around, are having a hard time keeping up with the times. I remember when Luca and I started going out together; we had to conform to the strict rules and regulations of those days. I was quite an exception because I was working and I had an important job. As a public relations representative, the first in Italy, I was building an image for TWA, and when Luca and I decided to get married, our friends commented, "Giovanna, you don't have to work anymore."

I would say, "I have no intention of quitting!"

Everybody was shocked. "Then why are you getting married if he can't afford to keep a wife?" they asked.

My answer: "Times are changing. I plan to do it all, get married, have a family, and work. I will certainly hire helpers (maid, cook, nanny), and I hope to make a go of it."

It wasn't easy, and many of my so-called friends were green with envy, but we turned out to be a perfect combination, my gorgeous, jealous Sicilian husband and me. I'm not even going to try to list all my faults—I have plenty but not enough space to list them all. Of course, we had our ups and downs, and these little crises helped to bond us together all the more. We nearly made it to celebrate our fortieth wedding anniversary in 1988.

So what was the reason for our happy marriage?

First of all, we had to work on it, the "living together." Luca never saw me with curlers in my hair or cream on my face or wearing an old housedress. So what is the secret? One bed and separate bathrooms! I'm not kidding!

But back to the beginnings of my career at TWA.

On March 1, 1947, I showed up at the TWA office on Via Barberini in Rome to attend a course in ticketing because I wanted to become a flight hostess. I happened to be the only female among five young men, and one of those men was Luca Salvadore, who, two years later, became my husband. I was trying to be friendly, so I said to Luca, "We've already met." I was referring to a ping-pong tournament that I had organized a couple of years before while I was working at the American Red Cross—GIs against the Rome ping-pong team.

Luca looked me up and down and announced, "Never laid eyes on you." I was about to explode in annoyance, but instead I decided to make him pay for it. Every time he tried to date me, I would happily accept and then show up at the appointed place with several of the boys from our ticketing class.

I passed the exams, together with the five young men. Being the only female, my male colleagues spoilt me, and finally I was beginning to enjoy life after those terrifying war years. I went out with all the boys until Luca learned his lesson and behaved in a more civilized manner toward me. After that, it didn't take Luca (and me) much more time to decide that we were made for each other and that we should start making wedding plans.

We both came from old-fashioned families that believed we should go through the ropes. This meant formal engagement, meeting of the parents, Catholic Church wedding, white gown, reception, honeymoon, and then a perfect life together. In the two years we had known each other, Luca had come up in the ranks at TWA and had become sales manager for the company in Italy, while I was appointed the public relations representative in Italy—I was actually the first press representative in the country, male or female.

I had already worked as a ground hostess for TWA, and I had hoped to become a flight hostess. Impossible! I didn't have an American passport, but I did have a journalistic background. My grandfather, my father, and my brothers, all the men in my family, had been correspondents for Italian newspapers from abroad, and I was fluent in English. So I was chosen to represent TWA in Italy.

Rome had become the most popular, sought-after destination in Europe, and Hollywood had discovered that the art of filmmaking was flourishing in Italy. Rome became known as Hollywood on the Tiber. Italian movie director Roberto Rossellini with his masterpiece, *Rome, Open City,* and Vittorio De Sica with *Bicycle Thief* were among the first to be introduced to the American public. The era of realism had started and I had to be trained to fill the job as the first woman PR executive in Italy.

During my TWA days I would receive calls from passengers who wanted special treatment because they were friends of Howard Hughes. In the beginning I fell for it, but the requests were so many that I learned to distinguish the phonies. Or so I thought.

Then one day I got a call from a certain Glenn McCarthy, who introduced himself as a friend of Howard Hughes. "Sure," said I, but I didn't give him the time of day. Shortly thereafter, I got a call from Los Angeles. It was Johnny Meyer, Howard Hughes's public relations man, asking me to look out for Glenn McCarthy, a friend of Howard Hughes. Well, I did everything to make up for being rude and from then on I asked to be informed when there was someone as important as McCarthy, the entrepreneur, coming in.

It is hard to find anybody under sixty who remembers the legendary Texan Glenn McCarthy, although his picture appeared on the cover of *Time* magazine. McCarthy came from a modest family, but at the age of eight, he was already working as a water boy, bringing water to roughnecks in the oil fields for fifty cents a day. He ultimately became a wildcatter and drilled for oil in Texas. After many attempts, he struck oil in the 1930s; during the 1940s he established eleven new oil fields. Calling him rich is an understatement.

It is said that every week seemed to bring a new McCarthy initiative. Let's forget about the many projects he started and concentrate on the building of the Shamrock Hotel in Houston. McCarthy spent $21 million on the hotel, which was an unfathomable amount at the time. The year was 1949 and the hotel inaugural was to take place, if possible, on March 17, Saint Patrick's Day. McCarthy was of Irish descent and that is why the hotel was named Shamrock. It was to be the largest hotel in the world. (When asked his opinion of the Shamrock Hotel, Frank Lloyd Wright said that he had always wondered how the inside of a jukebox looked!)

The media went to town writing about McCarthy, who became known as the Wildcatter. Thousands of invitations were sent out for the hotel's inaugural, and all of Hollywood attended. The evening of the opening, a crowd of five thousand people had surrounded the hotel. By dusk the limousines started to arrive, disgorging the celebrities.

Errol Flynn was the first to get out and he waved to the cheering crowd, followed by Ginger Rogers, Van Johnson, Van Heflin, Pat O'Brien, Dinah Shore, Frank Sinatra, Dorothy Lamour, and many, many more—except for one. Howard Hughes.

The event was a mob scene, and an utter disaster. The people inside couldn't get out and the people outside couldn't get in. The rooms were taken apart by rowdy revelers, and the damages were immense. The *Houston Chronicle* described the opening as "bedlam in diamonds."

After that, when I was in Houston, I stayed at the downtown Rice Hotel, spending most of my time there with the Holcombes. Oscar Holcombe, an icon of the city, served as mayor for more than twenty years. Holcombe was also a board member of TWA, so I had always tried to go out of my way to entertain him and his wife when they were in Rome.

I loved Rome in those years, and I still do. I studied all about its more than five hundred churches, its museums, its monuments, its buildings, and plenty more, so that I could become a guide for the TWA "visiting firemen." If my Luca hadn't moved to Milan with the family, I would probably still be in Rome, pointing out the sights to anyone who was interested.

But back to the Shamrock. It was located outside Houston, and it was inconvenient, and it was losing money when Hilton stepped in and bought it in less than five years after that grand opening. But this seemed not to faze McCarthy; the flamboyant tycoon went on to build other projects.

It was at this time, about 1952, when novelist Edna Ferber's book *Giant* was published. Later it became a movie starring Elizabeth Taylor, with James Dean as the leading man, Jett Rink. It is said that Jett Rink was based on Glenn McCarthy.

As a PR rep, I had no idea what the job actually entailed, but I was so eager to learn that I worked hard on the job. I love people and I went out of my way to help the press with its stories, so everything went fairly smoothly. At first I was not aware that my ultimate "boss" was Howard Hughes (who at the time owned 78 percent of the airline). But once the news of his involvement got out, and once word started to spread that Rome was becoming the center of the movie world, exciting things started to happen.

So many celebrities are completely forgotten in today's world: a perfect example is Stanley Baker, the Welsh actor and film producer.

Stanley was a close friend and drinking companion of Richard Burton. He was knighted in 1976 but did not live to receive the honor officially at Buckingham Palace. He died at the age of 48.

For a long time he had been cast in the movies as a villain, until he was spotted by Laurence Olivier and given a role in *Richard III.* He is remembered for his part in *Zulu* alongside Michael Caine. This was when he formed his own production company. Some of his last projects were the miniseries *How Green Was My Valley,* in 1975, and a BBC adaptation of *Robinson Crusoe.* He came from a coal-mining background, started on the stage, and was somewhat rough-and-tumble, like Burton. He was quite distinctive, with his craggy good looks, and highly accomplished as well.

I met Stanley in Rome, where he spent a lot of time, and once, when he was booked on TWA, he asked me to accompany him to the airport. Happy to oblige, I picked him up and sat with him in the VIP lounge waiting for his flight to be announced.

A stray paparazzo sneaked into the lounge and snapped a photo of Baker and me. For once I did not mind this intrusion, because I made sure that I would get a copy of the image. I have to confess at this point that I always admired Stanley Baker. He was a very attractive guy, and I was not the only one to think so. It was quite tragic when he died so prematurely.

Exception to the rule of long-forgotten luminaries of the era, however, can be made for Howard Hughes, who became known in the late 1940s and early 1950s as the richest man in the world. No one ever forgot Howard Hughes.

Hughes behaved very strangely, spending the last years of his life as a complete recluse. His name alone conjures a host of images: Hollywood . . . playboy . . . adventurous pilot . . . spendthrift businessman. Today he is remembered with the Howard Hughes Medical Institute, America's second-largest philanthropy, behind only the Bill and Melinda Gates Foundation. Not a bad legacy for a playboy spendthrift! History may begin to remember Howard as a great, if accidental, patron of science.

We all remember him for different reasons. He was a billionaire and he inherited a fortune from his father, who owned the Hughes Tool Company. No matter how much money Howard Hughes squandered in movies, aircraft (including building TWA), and electronics, he always emerged on top. He even designed the Constellation, which TWA kept flying while other airlines had moved on to jets.

Hughes was also known as an escort to some of the most beautiful women, mostly actresses, such as Jean Harlow, Katharine Hepburn, Ginger Rogers, Ava Gardner, and Jean Peters.

Many are aware that he bought the RKO Studios (one of the most important film studios in the Golden Age of Hollywood) and that from 1941 to 1943 he produced and directed the movie *The Outlaw,* starring Jane Russell's bosom, for which he actually designed a brassiere. We must not forget that Howard Hughes was an engineer, and in that case he certainly did a great engineering job. The bra became "the topic" of conversation, followed in detail by the press and gossip columnists.

The movie was censored and declared unacceptable. Finally Noah Dietrich, Hughes's right-hand man, obtained permission from Cardinal Francis Spellman to release the film. Certainly no other movie of those days received such a publicity campaign. But when it was finally released, the moviegoers who rushed to see what was so scandalous were very disappointed, because there was nothing in it to shock the audience. Still, I remember when *The Outlaw* was dubbed in Italian and released after World War II. It was called *Il Mio Corpo Ti Scalderà (My Body Will Warm You Up).* It was a big hit in Italy!

Today, more people may recognize the name Howard Hughes thanks to the movie *The Aviator,* starring Leonardo DiCaprio as Hughes and Cate Blanchett as Katharine Hepburn, one of Hughes's heartthrobs. I enjoyed it, although to my mind many important parts of the story were left out.

But back to my personal life. My parents knew Luca very well because he would accompany me home every evening and join us at the dinner table. On the other hand, I had never met Luca's parents. As his fiancée, I was, at last, officially invited to meet my future in-laws at their house in Rome. I confess that I was quite nervous because Luca's mother was German, and from his description of her she sounded quite demanding.

When we arrived at the house, the whole family was waiting for us, and my future mother-in-law didn't give me time to settle down. She kept me standing while she sat in her favorite armchair and started to cross-examine me.

First question: "Do you play bridge?"

"No, ma'am. My job keeps me so busy that I have had no time to learn."

"Of course," she retorted, "you know that Luca loves to play bridge; it is his favorite pastime. But of course, you know how to cook."

And again I replied, "No, ma'am. My job keeps me so busy."

"Obviously," she said, "but you know that Luca is a gourmet and food is very important for him."

There were other questions that I don't remember. I only wanted to back out the door and run away. I was practically in tears when Luca's father, a handsome and gracious Sicilian gentleman, took me by the hand into his studio and said, "I think Luca is very lucky, and I can tell that the two of you will get along famously. But I must warn you that he is quite a gambler, so I suggest that you pick up his monthly salary and give him a weekly allowance. "

I was still quite shaken when we left Luca's house. I exploded at my fiancé and said, "I am ready to call it quits," at which point Luca said to me, "This mauve dress you are wearing, where does it come from?"

"What do you mean?" I said. "I had it made especially for this evening to meet your parents!"

"All right," said Luca. "I might as well tell you. Mother can't stand the color mauve!"

As you now know, Luca and I enjoyed a very happy married life together, which lasted nearly forty years. But at the beginning of my romance with Luca, his mother and I didn't quite see eye-to-eye. Later, when I got to know her well, I have to admit that I became quite fond of her.

A few months after my debut in the Salvadore family we started talking about our wedding. I forgot to mention that Luca had a brother one year younger than he was, named Andrea, and a sister who was ten years younger, named Aglaya, who doted upon Luca and seemed to accept me.

First of all we had to book the church, and this, according to tradition, had to be the parish church. I immediately made it known that I had already made arrangements with my Irish friend Father Hubert Quinn of Saint Isidore, the Irish Catholic church in Rome. How did we become friends, Father Quinn and I?

Every year on St Patrick's Day, March 17, I asked my colleagues from Ireland to send me baskets of shamrocks. TWA hostesses distributed the shamrocks to the Irish community in Rome. Father Quinn was so pleased with this gesture that he offered to marry Luca and me. I brought my Luca to meet Father Quinn, and once we got his approval we thought we had it all set.

Little did we know that we had to have a special dispensation to be married outside of our own parish. It wasn't easy, but eventually we got all the papers and went to the town hall for the civil marriage. On April 30, 1949, Luca and I became husband and wife. After the civil ceremony, we went to Father Quinn's church for a religious ceremony in front of our family and friends.

My mother took care of my trousseau, which consisted of hand-embroidered chiffon nightgowns (which was amusing because I only wear pajamas!).

The church held less than one hundred people. It was so beautiful, and I must say that we had a great turnout, so great that many of our friends were left outside the church located off the Via Veneto in Rome. Once the ceremony was over, we walked over to the Excelsior Hotel, where the reception took place.

We then left for our honeymoon, and although we had free tickets for any TWA destination, we ended up on Lake Maggiore. Luca's choice was Stresa, but we didn't remain long because after a couple of days we ran out of money . . . so we moved to a small pensione. Then I got a desperate call from the office: Ralph Damon, the new president of TWA, was arriving in Rome on his first visit. I was needed to show Mr. Damon around Rome and to throw a cocktail party in his honor. In the late 1940s and, early 1950s everybody was in a cocktail mood, and I like to think that this was the beginning of *La Dolce Vita.*

I never let on, but Mr. Damon did Luca and me a great favor by turning up at that time. We had run out of money, and because we had no place to go, we knocked on my parents' door and asked if we could stay until we found an apartment. We stayed for a year and a half, until my parents threw us out and suggested that we start setting up a home and having children.

I just want to mention that Mr. Damon was one of the nicest gentlemen I ever met. He was a true New Englander. He always traveled in a tweed suit with two nylon shirts, which he washed out in turn every night.

Mr. Damon and I shared a private joke. While we were sightseeing and I was pointing out various antiquities such as the Colosseum, the Roman Forum, the Basilica of Maxentius, and so on, Mr. Damon interrupted me and asked, "But where is the Parthenon?" I was flabbergasted! I looked around, hoping to be inspired with an answer, and I blurted out, "Mr. Damon, you can't see it from here." Of course you couldn't; it was (and is) almost nine hundred miles away, in Athens.

"Next time," he answered. And with that he decided to cut short our sightseeing tour and go back to the office. A few days later I received a postcard of the Parthenon from Athens, and what did Mr. Damon write? "By golly, Jean, you were right!"

The late 1940s and the early 1950s were the most thrilling and glamorous years after a long, miserable, and scary war period. Howard Hughes had become not only the major shareholder in TWA, but he also owned RKO Cinema in Hollywood and was "directing traffic" to and from Rome on TWA.

The very first celebrities I met were Harold Russell, who had a role in *The Best Years of Our Lives,* the first big post-war movie, and Margaret O'Brien. Harold was a Canadian-American World War II veteran who had lost both hands during the war; he became one of only two non-professional actors ever to win an Academy Award. He also holds the unique honor of being the only person to receive two Academy Awards for the same role. Margaret O'Brien had starred as a child actress with Judy Garland in the movie *Meet Me in St. Louis.* She was only a child when I met her, and a lot younger than me, but she was a well-known film star and I was very nervous at the thought of meeting her: What would I say? It took me awhile to get rid of my shyness.

As time went by I became used to meeting celebrities, from prime ministers to movie stars, from Jawaharlal Nehru and Éamon de Valera to Arturo Toscanini, Luciano Pavarotti, and Yehudi Menuhin.

Among the most memorable celebrities I took care of were Louella Parsons, who was accompanied by her husband, Dr. Harry Martin, and actress Irene Dunne. Louella was really a good friend to Howard Hughes; she kept him out of her column, "Tell It to Louella," as much as possible. That made Hughes very happy because he did not want to be mentioned in the papers. Many a scoop she could have made never saw the light of day because of their friendship.

Hedda Hopper, another famous columnist of the day, thrived on Hollywood gossip and traveled with Jerome Zerbe, the society photographer of the legendary New York nightclub El Morocco. They came to cover the scene in Rome.

Other well-known journalists I got to know were Radie Harris, Cobina Wright, and Sheilah Graham. It was Sheilah who had assisted the ailing F. Scott Fitzgerald until his death in 1940. Their relationship was immortalized in her book *Beloved Infidel,* later made into a Hollywood movie.

Better known as Mr. Celebrity, Earl Blackwell, who introduced me to Rock Hudson, made friends with the most important people from his generation, such as Joan Crawford, Tyrone Power, Ronald and Nancy Reagan, and Winston Churchill. He created the world's foremost information bureau on celebrities with offices in New York, Hollywood, London, Paris, and Rome.

We worked well together. I kept him informed of important arrivals, and we often threw parties together that were the talk of the town— New York being the town. My parties were very modest, while Blackwell turned parties into events. We all remember when he engaged Marilyn Monroe to sing "Happy Birthday" to President John F. Kennedy in 1962 at Madison Square Garden. In 1967 he organized a fabulous costume ball in Venice, which will go down as the party of the century.

It was through Blackwell that I also encountered Eugenia Sheppard, who, at that time was a syndicated fashion writer and columnist for eighty or more newspapers. I remember reading her column in the late 1950s and 1960s in the *Herald Tribune*. She was a great supporter of the designer Valentino and implemented his rise to the top of the fashion industry; no one dared disagree with her positive assessment of the young designer.

And then there was Walter Winchell. He was the number one gossip columnist from the 1930s until the 1950s. Those were the days when Leonard Lyons, Earl Wilson, and Louis Sobol, on the East Coast, together with Louella Parsons and Hedda Hopper on the West Coast, were read avidly. Because I represented TWA public relations, I would keep all of these columnists informed of the goings-on in Rome.

Rome was the city where celebrities lived *La Dolce Vita*. Via Veneto was an ideal meeting place, with its deluxe hotels and open-air cafés where you could sit all day sipping a cappuccino and watching the world go by.

There were many trattorias for lunch and dinner, always in the same area and mostly in the open. Until late at night you could sit outside, or you could drop in at "Bricktop's" to have a drink and sometimes even stay until morning, when "Bricktop" would prepare breakfast for her friends—maybe Frank Sinatra and his group, maybe some other famous crowd. Always on the lookout, the paparazzi would spend the night outside "Bricktop's," hoping to photograph the celebrities. Ada "Bricktop" Smith was an African-American self-described "saloonkeeper" who owned the nightclub Chez Bricktop in Paris from 1924-1961, as well as clubs in Mexico City and Rome.

And finally there was Westbrook Pegler, considered the most controversial political right-wing American columnist of all time, who wrote for King Features Syndicate. As the story goes, he never had a kind word for anybody except for his wife, Julia.

Pegler's contact in Rome was Michael Chinigo, the head of the International News Service (I.N.S.). Luca and I went out of our way to keep them both happy.

And then one night Luca got a call, "Come quickly! Julia died!"

We didn't ask for any explanations; we just rushed to Pegler's hotel, The Flora. When we reached the Peglers' room, accompanied by the hotel manager, we got a confirmation that Julia Pegler was dead. Naturally, Westbrook was beside himself and even attempted suicide in front of us by throwing himself out of the window. Finally the doctor sedated him, and he was brought to another room.

Together with the Chinigos, we took turns keeping Pegler company until the funeral took place in Rome. Senator Barry Goldwater, another renowned right-winger, flew into Rome with Pegler's private secretary, Maud Towart, who took over making preparations and comforting Pegler. Ironically, without Julia at his side, Pegler mellowed, and four years after Julia's departure, he married Maud.

Once it became clear to the world at large that there was a new Rome public relations office that would service the world press on the comings and goings of celebrities, it didn't take long for the cream of the Manhattan columnists to follow suit by traveling to Rome. As the PR ambassador, I came to know them all. In those days, PR was much more of a collaborative effort with columnists than it is today. We all worked together to place the stories that kept the public entertained; rather working at odds with the columnists ferreting out gossip and the PR people trying to keep certain facts under wraps.

I particularly remember Leonard Lyons, who wrote the column "The Lyons' Den" for the *New York Post.* He often went out of his way to help me. He took me with him on his rounds to all the hot nightspots such as El Morocco and the Stork Club and introduced me to all the celebrities. He was known as the greatest table-hopper of all time.

I met his wife, Sylvia, and their four sons, and we became such close friends that the Lyons boys often stayed with my family when in Rome. And Andrea, my son, was also a guest of the Lyons family in New York City, in the landmark building where they lived. Their neighbors included Mike Nichols and Rock Hudson.

One time I arrived in New York (it probably was in 1968), and when I talked to the Lyonses, I was invited to attend a Sunday brunch, "just the family," as Sylvia put it. Come Sunday I got into my little black dress; I wore my pearls and my black mink coat. This ensemble was a typical Italian "uniform," according to Bill Blass, the American couturier.

I showed up at the Lyons's apartment, and guess who opened the door? Mary Hemingway, the writer's fourth wife, who welcomed me by saying, "You must be Jean Salvadore. You're dressed like an Italian."

She ushered me in, and I was introduced to no less than Marc Chagall himself. Unfortunately I could not keep up a conversation because Yiddish was not a familiar language to me, and he and Sylvia were speaking in Yiddish. Sylvia was fluent in Yiddish, and as our hostess, she became our official translator. What a wonderful experience.

The party was fairly small, and as I looked around the room I spotted, among others, David Douglas Duncan, Picasso's favorite photographer, and New York Senator Jacob Javits. What a day—I will never forget it!

Earl Wilson was another columnist I enjoyed. He always referred to his wife Rosemary as "my beautiful wife," no matter what the context. The last time I saw him was at my TWA farewell party at the 21 Club in New York City in 1966.

I wish I could say the same about Walter Winchell! He was notorious because he was so powerful and used it to the max. He could make or break a PR career in a moment because it was known he had no regard for anyone else's status or career. I know that his biography has been written and distributed in all the English-speaking countries, notwithstanding the fact that I doubt whether the younger generation knows who he was. In the 1950s I happened to have fed him gossip tidbits about the stars who were putting Rome on the map. This was a request that came directly from Howard Hughes's office. Winchell was considered an institution, and his gossip column was read by an estimated 35 million readers and radio fans. His biography has even been translated into Italian and was on the bestseller list when it was published.

Soon the California studios discovered that movies could be made in Italy on a minimal budget. One of the very first productions was the epic *Quo Vadis.* The locations were in and around Rome, as it was about the conflict of Christianity and the corruption of the Roman Empire. The scenes were gigantic, with thousands of extras picked from the streets.

On the spur of the moment, and with the assistance of Adele Baracchi, who worked with me in the public relations office of TWA for more than ten years, I organized a cocktail party that went down in history.

The year was 1950, and because the filming of *Quo Vadis* was under way, we invited the producers and the entire cast and crew. These included Mervyn LeRoy, Deborah Kerr, and Robert Taylor (who asked to be excused because he was not wearing a dark suit, having come directly from the set). Approximately 500 people arrived at the party. Those were the days when TWA, the first airline to cross the Atlantic, could ask for the moon, because it had initiated a direct link between the United States and Italy, spurring tourism, which was to become an economic mainstay for the country.

Shortly after the event, Adele left TWA and started a family, and I believe to this day many ex-TWA regular passengers will remember her.

I became friendly with the director of the movie, Mervyn LeRoy, who invited me to bring some of my VIP passengers to the set. He suggested that I should bring them on the days that they would be filming the Christians being nailed to the cross. He said they would be paid as extras. Imagine returning home to tell your friends that you had taken part in a major Hollywood movie—despite the sensitive subject matter.

During my time at TWA, I seemed to spend more time at the airport greeting arriving celebrities than I spent in my office in Rome. At first it was Ciampino Airport, which was only twenty minutes away from the center of Rome, so it was not an inconvenience, but when the airport moved to Fiumicino that became a different story.

This is when my husband Luca and I decided to buy a villa in Fregene in 1962, the fashionable seaside resort close to Fiumicino. The villas at that time were very inexpensive because people did not like the idea of being practically attached to the airport. For us, the location was perfectly convenient, and in later years, as it developed into something of a hotspot, we realized we had made a smart move.

I got into the habit of meeting the morning arrivals at the airport and taking my VIPs to Fregene for a lunch on the beach, then into town. I remember that Jean Peters was one of these lucky recipients of my hospitality.

Jean arrived when she was the fiancée of Howard Hughes. For some reason or other Hughes had decided he didn't want to alienate the powers that be at Twentieth Century Fox, so Jean was in Rome to film *Three Coins in the Fountain,* which would be the last film she would make before marrying Hughes.

Breaking her contract by marrying Hughes immediately would entail a huge fine, although it was probably what Jean Peters wanted to do.

Hughes didn't want to pay the fine, or marry immediately, so he made sure that she was pampered by everyone on the set well beyond her status as a star at the time. So I was told to book her into the finest suite available at the Grand Hotel, the very best hotel in Rome at the time. I was also instructed to send Jean a hundred dollars' worth of flowers, anonymously, without a card, each day. After a few days I was at loss as to what else I could do to make her happy. With the money I had already spent, we could have started our own flower shop.

At some point Jean figured out I was sending the flowers for H.H., as we called him, and begged me not to send any more flowers because her suite resembled a funeral parlor. Of course, feigning ignorance to the entire series of events, I said that I did not know what she was talking about. Finally I got a call from Los Angeles saying to stop the "flower promotion." I guess she went to a higher authority.

After that Jean and I got along famously, maybe because we were exactly the same age. She was a sweet, unassuming girl and in the end she did marry Howard Hughes, a union that lasted fourteen years. The marriage, however, didn't work out. Many years later when I was visiting friends in Los Angeles, I was told that she had died in 2000. Apparently her divorce settlement was not favorable and she died penniless.

Howard Hughes's only living relations were his aunts, Martha Houston and Mrs. Fred Lummis, and when they visited I was instructed that they were to stay at the Hassler, another of Rome's finest hotels. You would think they had stepped out of the Frank Capra movie *Arsenic and Old Lace,* they were so unimposing.

When I welcomed them at the airport they immediately exclaimed, "That naughty boy!" meaning Howard Hughes. "He shouldn't have disturbed you." Nevertheless, I spent several days taking them shopping and sightseeing and giving them the VIP treatment.

I never met Richard Avedon in person, but I came to know Theo Graham, his very first model. Again, Fregene was the point of contact. I met Theo on the beach of Fregene, near our villa. Those were the days when it was fashionable to spend the day sunning, lunching on the catch of the day, and returning to Rome to dress for an evening on the town, stopping at some little trattoria and then on to Via Veneto to watch the world go by. This was part of *La Dolce Vita.*

Theo and I became good friends, and the beach we chose was called Toni's, after the owner, a fisherman. We all had cabanas, including Marcello Mastroianni, Kirk Douglas, Federico Fellini, and Rossano Brazzi, among others. Theo reminded me of Audrey Hepburn: tall and slim, chestnut brown hair, an oval face, high cheekbones, a long, slender neck, and great elegance.

When Avedon and Theo started working together in New York, she was only nineteen years old and he was twenty-one; he had originally hired her as his office assistant. The war had just ended, and their relationship began when she knocked on Avedon's door looking for a job. He was at the beginning of his career and he worked his way up to become one of the top fashion photographers in the world. She worked her way up to become a runway model of some repute. Their meeting and intersection came at an important moment in fashion history because it involved many greats before they were famous: Avedon, Carmel Snow, Christian Dior at a turning point in his career, and the famed art director Alexey Brodovitch.

As the story goes, Avedon had threatened Snow, famed editor of the American magazine *Harper's Bazaar,* that he would "defect" to *Vogue* if he wasn't sent to Paris to cover the shows. So, headed back in 1949, he insisted on his choice of two models for the trip, instead of the customary one, to help "inspire his creativity." Dorian Leigh accepted immediately, but his other choice, twenty-two-year-old Theo, took a bit more convincing. It was a shining moment in Graham's career, but she quit modeling soon thereafter.

Theo died in 1996, and recently Theo's son, Enrico Carlo Saraceni, came across a cardboard box with hundreds of photos of his mother, who was Christian Dior's favorite model. In 2009, their relationship as artist and model was fully chronicled in an exhibition shown in Rome at the Capitolini Museums and the French Academy-Villa Medici-Rome.

Ultimately Carmel Snow would become the most powerful fashion arbiter in the United States. Even after she retired in 1957, she continued to cover the shows. She was a tiny woman, but she commanded attention and kept everybody on their toes.

José Iturbi, Arturo Toscanini, and Jawaharlal Nehru all made appearances, and I was there to greet them, too.

José Iturbi was a sublime pianist. He was also a small man with a big ego and he had a flair for publicity. Born in Valencia, Spain, he began playing the piano and supporting himself financially when he was only seven years old. Ultimately, he became a movie star, a composer, and, in 1950, the conductor of the Valencia Philharmonic Orchestra. He will always be remembered for playing the piano score in *A Song to Remember,* the wonderful 1945 film biography of the life of Frédéric Chopin, starring Cornel Wilde.

Whenever Iturbi flew TWA we were advised to go all out for him. I was impressed by how he handled himself. He was a born PR man.

I met conductor Arturo Toscanini through mutual friends who put me in touch with Wally Castelbarco, daughter of the conductor. She was accompanying her father to the United States, but because he had a fear of flying she enlisted me to assist with her temperamental father.

At that time, Toscanini was considered the greatest conductor in the world. Born in Parma, Italy, he had become an orchestra conductor only by chance. After graduating at the age of eighteen from Parma's Royal School of Music, by nineteen he was engaged as principal cellist and assistant chorus master of an Italian opera company that was to tour South America. One evening in Rio de Janeiro, Toscanini was called upon at the last moment to replace the ensemble's regular conductor in a performance of the opera *Aida,* which he led without musical score and from memory. Thus began one of the most extraordinary careers in the history of musical performance.

Although at first he welcomed the Fascist regime, in 1931 he refused to play their hymn "Giovinezza" and the national anthem. For this he was badly beaten by the Black Shirts. This was when he decided to emigrate to the United States, where he was offered the position of principal conductor for the New York Philharmonic. He lived there until the end of his life. In 1946 he returned to Italy for the last time, to direct a concert at La Scala, which was a triumph.

And suddenly here it was 1948, and I had my instructions: "Humor the maestro."

I tried various arguments to calm him about his trip, but to no avail. I would have enjoyed smoking a cigarette, but I was sure that the maestro would not approve. So I always had a few pieces of candy on hand for times when I could not smoke.

I turned around and asked the maestro if he would care for a piece of candy. His face lit up, and he gave me a big, broad smile and helped himself to the candy. I looked over to his daughter, who winked at me. From then on we had a most enjoyable time.

Jawaharlal Nehru was difficult to entertain in an entirely different way. He was essentially silent. To this day I have kept a photo of us together, fearing no one would believe that he and I actually walked together from the terminal of Leonardo da Vinci-Fuimicino Airport, near Rome.

As the PR rep for TWA, I went to the airport to make sure that Nehru was well received. His flight was only making a stopover in Rome on the way to Bombay, but the flight was late, and it arrived in the middle of the night.

As I always tried to be prepared, I informed myself on Nehru's life: Educated in England, he spent fourteen years in British prisons for his activities as a leader of the Indian Independence movements, then finished his studies at Cambridge University and returned to India to become Mahatma Gandhi's chief disciple. I don't remember our specific conversation, but I do remember being utterly charmed by his gentle manners and his soft voice.

In the photo record of this event, taken over fifty years ago, I look like I don't know where to look, and although I'm generally never at loss for words, I was not at ease finding myself in the middle of the night with one of the great minds of this world.

Also Nehru looks seems embarrassed—probably because we had no topics of conversation!

In 1948 when I had just been appointed as the full-time PR rep for TWA, it was almost immediately pronounced that I would make my first trip to the USA. I was only twenty-two years old.

Gordon Gilmore, the vice president of PR in New York, booked me in at the Plaza Hotel, which was breathtaking in its splendor. I rested up after a twenty-five-hour flight and got ready to go to my first cocktail party.

For the occasion Gordon sent me a corsage, which consisted of chrysanthemums. I was horrified because in Italy this flower is to be found principally at funerals and cemeteries. So I didn't wear the corsage, much to the big boss's chagrin. I guess I started off on the wrong foot.

When we arrived at the cocktail party—I think it was in the Plaza—it resembled a scene out of *Breakfast at Tiffany's*. The room was packed and everybody was dressed to the nines. The ladies wore elegant cocktail dresses, while the men were in their dark suits.

The room was so crowded that those smoking, and they were the majority, held their cigarettes above their heads and tried to balance their drinks in the other hand. Everyone had identical cocktails. I soon found out that the drink was known as a martini. I had never tasted one before, and I thought it would be wiser not to start.

Next everybody was offering me a cigarette. I refused because I had never smoked. During the war, my mother was the only one who would sit at the table and smoke. She would say, "I'm not hungry," then "smoke" her meal so that her family would receive a bigger portion of food. My father, on the other hand, gave up smoking in exchange for one glass of wine.

At some point Gordon took me aside and said, "I'm afraid you will not become a good PR rep if you don't learn to drink and smoke." With that he gave me a martini glass filled with water and decorated with an olive. "The smoking will come later," he pronounced. Sure enough, I learned to puff away and for some fifty-odd years I rather enjoyed it. I gave it up only when I was expecting and nursing. In recent years, I found I was spending so much time in hospitals that I finally had to stop smoking altogether.

I believe the birth of the paparazzi took place on March 20, 1949, when the one and only Ingrid Bergman stepped off a TWA plane in Rome and was immediately surrounded by dozens of photographers who went absolutely crazy as they chanted, "Ingrid, Ingrid!" I tried to shield her from the assault, but she towered over me and I was afraid that we would be trampled to death.

It was pitch dark because the flight had been delayed several times, and instead of arriving in the early afternoon it landed in the middle of the night. Fortunately the policemen were able to rescue Ingrid

The author, Jean Govoni, and her fiancé, Luca Salvadore, just before their marriage in 1949.

Left: Jean and Luca Salvadore on their wedding day, April 30, 1949.

Above: Family dog Jasper secures the perimeter of the bassinet of the Salvadore's firstborn, son Andrea, in 1952.

Pianist José Iturbi (left) at Ciampino Airport in Rome with the author *(center)* and TWA stationmaster Memphis Cole, June 1948.

Alberto Moravia *(center)*, greeted by the author and Marta Maltseff, TWA ground hostess. Note Rome's Borghese Gardens in the background.

Irish premier in 1948, Éamon de Valera, arrives at Ciampino Airport.

The author's first star encounter was with child actress Margaret O'Brien, who is seen here at Ciampino just before she departs for Paris.

Ingrid Bergman's arrival in Rome on March 19, 1949 caused a sensation. She was arriving in Rome to star in Roberto Rossellini's movie *Stromboli*.

Actor and comedian Danny Kaye arrives at Rome's Ciampino Airport in November, 1978.

Robert Taylor arrives at a cocktail party, in what he thinks is too casual attire, having come directly from the set of *Quo Vadis* which was filming in Rome in 1951. Bea Mazzarini and Ralph Damon, then president of TWA, greet him.

P.S. Wednesday, la bambola, la comprai a New York. Ero l'unica ad averla ed ora mi procuri un'inflazione, accidenti!

Above: The author with journalist Oriana Fallaci tour Manhattan during their time off from an Italian press junket in 1953.

Right: The group assembled in Washington, DC include Guglielmo Biraghi, columnist and President of the Venice Film Festival, the author, Lamberto Sechi from Rizzoli Publications; Oriana Fallaci; and Paolo Monelli, Sr., journalist.

Following: The Salvadore family at home in 1960: Jean, Andrea, Claudia, and Luca.

Claudia on her First Holy Communion Day with her mother *(left)* and her godmother, Gabriella Gisci, 1961.

The entire family celebrates Claudia's First Communion, from left to right: Jean, Andrea, Claudia, and Luca.

Left: Elizabeth Taylor departing for Madrid on the TWA Constellation, September 1953.

Above: Jean Peters, departing from Rome to return to Hollywood in 1953, after appearing in the movie, *Three Coins in the Fountain.* This was the last movie she made before marrying Howard Hughes.

Frank Sinatra and wife Ava Gardner on arrival from Madrid at the end of 1953. Their marriage created something of a scandal and elicited great interest from the paparazzi.

In 1960 Silvana Mangano, famed for her performance in *Bitter Rice,* was filming a movie called *Jovanka e le Altre,* which necessitated a very short haircut and high fashion.

Famed Italian conductor Arturo Toscanini arrives in Rome in 1948.

Many travelers from the States began their journeys in Rome and then traveled on to Paris, as did Gary Cooper, his wife and daughter, in 1953 as well as Lauren Bacall and husband Humphrey Bogart, in 1954.

In 1954 Douglas Fairbanks, Jr. departed for Madrid, after causing a sensation during his visit. At the time he was one of the most important and famous actors in the world.

Two days earlier, on July 18, 1954 William Holden, an even greater heartthrob, arrived to thrilled fans and the TWA staff at Rome's Ciampino Airport.

Audrey Hepburn and husband Mel Ferrer traveled without entourage or fanfare to Paris after Hepburn finished filming *Roman Holiday,* in 1955.

Empress Soraya of Persia and her Iranian Embassy escort departed Rome for Madrid. She was often mistaken for Sophia Loren because of her exotic beauty.

Hedda Hopper, whom always seemed to be talking, with photographer Jerome Zerbe arrive in Rome, where there was much gossip to be had at the time.

Following: Actress Irene Dunne, columnist Louella Parsons, and Jean Govoni meet at Ciampino. Note that all the women, in the dead of summer, wear gloves.

Actor Edmond Purdom is greeted by Jean Salvadore when he arrives back to Rome where he had relocated. Purdom married actress Linda Christian after she was divorced from Tyrone Power.

Harold Russell was one of the first two visitors greeted by the author in her public relations position for TWA. Margaret O'Brien, the child actress, was the other.

Jawaharlal Nehru, the first prime minister of India, also known as Pandit Nehru, arrives with strong airport security and is escorted by the author, who was quite intimidated by his high intellectual standing.

Stanley Baker, the Welsh actor and film producer, and the author share a moment before a flight in the TWA lounge at Rome's Ciampino airport.

In 1962 Richard Burton took a day's leave from shooting Cleopatra to travel to Paris for a cameo in *The Longest Day*.

Sheila Graham, well-known Hollywood columnist, was born in London and went on stage to become known as "London's most beautiful showgirl." Here, in 1955, she arrives in Rome at the time her book, *Beloved Infidel,* was published. The book chronicles her romance with F. Scott Fitzgerald, which lasted four years and with whom she remained until his death in 1940.

Donna Ida Einaudi, wife of the President of the Italian Republic, being interviewed by Faye Hammond of The Los Angeles Times, in 1954, at the Quirinale Palace. The author acted as interpreter.

Gregory Peck is still considered one of the great Hollywood stars of all time. Here, in 1953, he came to Rome to star in *Roman Holiday* with Audrey Hepburn and it was here, in Rome, that he met Veronique Passani, the French journalist who became his second wife.

Left: In 1953 the author met Montgomery Clift at the Rome airport, but kept a distance as he was known to be uncooperative with the press. He didn't want to be treated like a "star."

Above: In 1950, Gina Lollobrigida and her husband, Milko Skofich, are greeted by the author.

Kirk Douglas was photographed during the time he romanced Italian actress Anna Maria Pietrangeli, a liaison that did not last long.

Errol Flynn arrives at Ciampino Airport in 1949.

Shirley MacLaine disembarks in Rome in a "matching" Chanel suit as that worn by the author.

Eddie Fisher arrives to check on the situation between his wife, Elizabeth Taylor, and Richard Burton when the filming of *Cleopatra* was underway.

The author and Robert Ruark stroll the streets of Rome in 1952.

Sophia Loren always caused a sensation when arriving in Rome and received premier attention from crew and staff.

and escort her to a car, where Roberto Rossellini waited inside for her. Finally the nightmare of Ingrid Bergman's arrival was over and I could go home and sleep.

The next day I got a call from Los Angeles to find out how the divine actress was welcomed by the Roman press.

The term "paparazzi" originated in Federico Fellini's 1960 film *La Dolce Vita*. It comes from a character in the film named Paparazzo (played by Walter Santesso), a news photographer. It came to mean those photographers who take candid shots of celebrities caught unaware. Some say Fellini took the name from an Italian dialect that describes a particularly annoying noise, that of a buzzing mosquito.

It had been a slow build-up, which, according to history, started when Ingrid Bergman, who lived in Los Angeles, saw Rossellini's film, *Open City*. She was so taken by it that she immediately wrote to Rossellini expressing all her admiration and hoping that she might one day appear in one of his movies. Apparently she signed off on the letter, otherwise written all in English, with a flourishing *"Ti amo"*—Italian for "I love you."

Upon receipt of this letter Rossellini wasted no time, and he flew to Los Angeles to meet Ingrid. It all happened so quickly that shortly after Rossellini returned I got word from Los Angeles that Ingrid Bergman was booked on a TWA flight to arrive in Rome on March 20, 1949, when she would begin work with Rossellini on the movie *Stromboli*. I was to go all out and alert the press, which I did immediately.

The first response came from Rossellini, who called me, infuriated. "Who gave you permission to advise the press of Ingrid Bergman's arrival?" he asked me.

"My Los Angeles office," I answered.

Apparently he was so furious because Anna Magnani, the number one Italian actress, was living in his suite at the Excelsior. The Excelsior was not only the most fashionable hotel in Rome, but also the one where most celebrities stayed. Including Ingrid Bergman.

That same night, when my Los Angeles contact called, I plucked up some courage and said, "Mr. Rossellini is real mad at me because I announced that Ingrid Bergman was arriving." Upon which I was told, "Young lady, make up your mind. Are you working for Howard Hughes or Roberto Rossellini?* Also, remind the maestro who is financing *Stromboli*." (*Stromboli*, by the way, ended up being a big flop.)

Finally we all calmed down, and while Roberto Rossellini and Ingrid Bergman were filming on the volcanic island of Stromboli, Anna Magnani and movie director William Dieterle were on the nearby volcanic island of Volcano filming *Volcano*. (Another flop.)

There were paparazzi and then there were photographers, the distinction being commerce versus artistry. I have always been fascinated by photography, and I met so many photographers that I could tell stories about them to fill a whole book. However, I think I should limit myself to those who left an everlasting impression on me.

The first big impression maker was Chim, who changed his name from Szymin to Seymour; his first name was David. However, all his friends knew him as Chim.

David Szymin was born in 1911 in Warsaw into a family of publishers. After studying printing in Leipzig and chemistry and physics at the Sorbonne in the 1930s, Chim stayed on in Paris, where he decided that photography was his passion when a family friend who owned a photo agency loaned him a camera. (Unfortunately in 1956, ten days before his forty-sixth birthday, Chim was killed by a bullet from an Egyptian sniper while shooting a story on an exchange of prisoners of war at the Suez Canal.)

In the early 1950s, Chim spent a lot of time visiting with me and my assistant, Adele. By the time I met him, he was already a well-known photographer, who, with Henri Cartier-Bresson and Robert Capa, had in 1947 founded Magnum Photos in Paris. He especially loved children, so when my son was born in 1952 he came to our home in the elegant Parioli district of Rome. As he had promised he would, he took photos of my baby, who was just 15 days old. Chim declared that newborn babies looked wizened.

The day he shot the photos of Andrea and myself along with our dog, Jasper, he went across the street afterwards, to the apartment of the Rossellini-Bergmans. There he photographed their newborn twins, Isotta and Isabella.

Somehow I was always finding photographers who took pictures of children and not the least of these was the Italian photographer Carlo

Bavagnoli, who kept a very low profile. Not many people are aware that my great friend Carlo is the only Italian to have achieved cover credit for photographs appearing on *LIFE* magazine.

In the early 1960s he took some great shots of my daughter, Claudia, and every time he visited with us he made a big fuss over her. Later I discovered that Claudia, barely six years old when the photos were taken, had proposed to Carlo! He patiently told her that they would talk about it when she grew up.

A few years later Carlo showed up with a very attractive young lady who was laden down with parcels destined for Claudia. Carlo had come to break the news to Claudia: He was about to get married. He explained that he was unable to wait for her to grow up, but he hoped she would be happy with all the gifts and, of course, she was invited to the wedding, where lots of sweets would be served.

Claudia seemed perfectly satisfied with the arrangements.

Also about that time, Luca's parents, who had moved to Caracas in Venezuela, were trying to get us to join them, but we had no intention of leaving Rome. Still, hoping to entice me and Luca, my father-in-law, an architect and engineer, was building a house for us.

Luca's parents kept insisting that we should at least make a trip to see what living in Caracas was like, so Luca got on a plane and visited his parents. He made a fast turnaround, and when he got home, he immediately said to me, "Don't worry, we will never leave Rome," as we both loved our lives there.

Luca had had to change planes in Lisbon because there were no direct flights to Caracas, and he had to stay overnight in a hotel to await the connecting flight the next day. Thinking that since he was staying overnight he might as well get a car, too, so he would then be able to drive to Cascais to say hello to King Umberto II, the former king of Italy, who was living in exile there. (I may have forgotten to mention that Luca was a monarchist, while I voted republican.)

Luca rang the doorbell, and the door was opened by the Marquis Falcone Lucifero, the equerry, who showed Luca into the king's studio. When Luca tried to reintroduce himself, Umberto stopped him by saying, "I know we have already met. I remember meeting you years ago at the Madrid airport. You were with your charming wife with the flaming red hair, who burst into tears when she saw me. I also was on the verge of crying. How could I ever forget this encounter? How is your wife?"

Hearing this story from Luca on his return from Caracas almost brought me to tears all over again, but for another reason. What had come over me? A liberal who fell apart upon meeting the monarch? I recalled that I was boohooing and between the sobs kept repeating, "Your Majesty!" I behaved like an emotional Italian!

I had sworn Luca to secrecy about this event at the time, worried that some of my friends might drop me as a result of this public show of obeisance. Now, in my mid-eighties, I can relax and not worry what my friends think of this crazed act of a subject to her throne!

Luca reported on the return from his visit that he had a pleasant chat with the ex-king, who had happily autographed a photo for us.

You can see that those first years at TWA were filled with fun and excitement . . . sometimes not always related entirely to the job front! But there was excitement at work, too.

We, meaning the various TWA PR representatives during that period, were me, of course, in Rome, Larry Langley in London, and Bernard Vannier in Paris. We would devise crazy promotions. One of my favorites was a tie-in with the production of the 1950s adventure film *The Crimson Pirate,* which was being filmed on the island of Ischia by director Robert Siodmak. (Ischia is a volcanic island in the Tyrrhenian Sea, at the northern end of the Gulf of Naples.)

We concocted a contest searching for a certain type of girl for a part in the movie. The director really wanted a specific girl who he had met . . . somewhere. He couldn't quite remember where. He only remembered that she had jet-black hair and deep blue eyes. And she had been wearing a uniform of some kind.

Telexes (in those days there were no computers) were sent out. It was a big beauty contest, open to any girl who could rustle up a uniform to wear.

Many girls sent in their photos and finally a certain Margaret Rowland—a TWA hostess!—was chosen. She had the required qualifications of black hair and blue eyes, and she looked very lovely in her hostess uniform. Big excitement! All the gossip columnists wrote up articles about the up and coming star. It was a sort of Cinderella story.

Margaret was a TWA ground hostess at the London airport, and she received a great send-off from her colleagues and an exuberant welcome by all the paparazzi when she arrived in Italy. Once she arrived in Rome, I took over and accompanied Margaret to Ischia.

The Crimson Pirate starred Burt Lancaster, then at the beginning of his acting career. He had been a touring acrobat, and had been chosen because of his stunning physique. Everyone welcomed Margaret, and she was immediately brought to the costume department and outfitted for the part. There were several rehearsals before filming would begin.

Margaret, looking very chipper, acted her part, which consisted of slicing a loaf of bread, but without any lines. We all watched, rapt, as Margaret repeated take after take. She must have sliced enough bread to feed a regiment! That evening a dinner was served in her honor, and the next day Margaret and I returned to Rome.

Of course, we were very anxious to see the movie . . . until we found out that Margaret's scene had been cut in the editing room.

Our budding starlet dressed again in her uniform and went back to the London airport. Nevertheless, she said that those few days had been like a fairy tale, and they had certainly provided some fun and great public relations for TWA.

The year 1950 was filled with excitement that included Gina Lollobrigida. I was full of admiration for Gina, who kept her name and refused to change it into something easier to spell or pronounce. Well, of course, some got into the habit of calling her Lollo, but that was it. She was not very tall, but she was beautifully proportioned and she resembled a Dresden porcelain. She first came on the scene in 1947, when she placed third in the Miss Italy contest.

She made two films in Italy with Vittorio De Sica, which catapulted her to stardom but were not seen outside of Italy. In one she played the part of a country girl, and she became famous almost overnight.

This is when I stepped in, having received notice from the Los Angeles office to "get Lollo on a plane to Los Angeles." Howard Hughes wanted to have her sign a contract for RKO. I helped her get a visa for the United States, but her husband, Milko Skofic, stateless and originally from Yugoslavia, was not granted a visa—so Gina had to leave alone. I went to her apartment and helped her pack.

She did go to Hollywood but realized soon enough that she was essentially a prisoner of Howard Hughes and returned to Italy as soon as possible. The problem, however, was that she had signed an exclusive contract with Hughes for America, so she was unable to make any movies without his consent in the United States until 1959. Once back in Italy, she made many films and became a beloved international star, all without any assistance from Howard Hughes.

In September 1959, I was invited by *LIFE* magazine to join Dodie Hamblin, the bureau chief in Rome, on the set of the film *Jovanka*, in Klagenfurt, Austria. I was assigned to Silvana Mangano, the busty Italian star who became director Luchino Visconti's favorite leading lady. She was without doubt a "grand dame," having been discovered by chance when she was given the major role in the movie *Bitter Rice;* the poster of her at work in a rice field created nothing short of a sensation. I was quite intimidated by her cool manners, and I was unable to get her to smile.

Totally aloof, Silvana was not devoured by the acting bug. But both Visconti and the photographer Tazio Secchiaroli worshipped the ground she trod on. Secchiaroli, one of the original paparazzo, became famous when he appeared in Fellini's *Dolce Vita.*

Mention the title *La Dolce Vita,* and you think of Federico Fellini, the best-known Italian movie director, who received so many accolades from his colleagues for his long career in the movies. His greatest movies, which made him famous worldwide, are *La Dolce Vita, 8 1/2* and *Amarcord.*

Fellini was born in 1920 to middle-class parents in Rimini, a town on the Adriatic Coast. Even as a child he spent his leisure time drawing and staging puppet shows. He enrolled in law school at the Rome University, but it is said that he never attended classes. He wanted, instead, to be a caricaturist and gag writer, not a lawyer. He wrote screenplays and assisted Roberto Rossellini in the filming of *Open City.* In his own movies, he had a very distinct style that was a blend of fantasy and baroque images.

Fellini was a big bulk of a man with a squeaky voice and a penchant for buxom women like Anita Ekberg, the star of his masterpiece, *La Dolce Vita.* The movie broke all box-office records because of a scandalous scene, in which the Turkish dancer, Haish Nana, improvised a striptease. Fellini was insulted and spat upon by an outraged patron, but this did not stop the crowds from queuing for hours to view this "immoral" movie.

Another memorable scene was Anita Ekberg wading fully dressed in the Fountain of Trevi with a young and bewildered Marcello Mastroianni.

We became neighbors to Fellini in Fregene. We used our small villa for weekends, while Fellini and his adorable wife Giulietta Masina, the leading lady in most of his movies, lived year-round in a fairly big house in the pine woods. We had many friends in common: journalists and columnists, photographers and just ordinary folks like ourselves.

Fellini was a genius, but very provincial, and the Hollywood on the Tiber phenomenon of the 1950s did not concern him.

It's almost hard to explain how exciting those TWA years were in every aspect.

For the first time, everybody—meaning royalty, statesmen, popes, movie stars—was traveling by air. Before World War II, you had to take a ship to cross the Atlantic. It took five to seven days to get there. Then, fortunately, the airlines, starting with TWA, took over.

One dominant figure in Irish politics and another prominent visitor to Rome on my watch was Éamon de Valera, the son of a Spanish musician and an Irish mother. He traveled often to Rome, and I always made it a point to meet him. It got so that we would greet each other like old friends.

I was fascinated by his life history. Sentenced to death for his political activities during the Easter Rising, an armed revolt in Dublin in 1916, he eventually escaped and left for the United States. Eventually de Valera became the first premier of Ireland and was in and out of office all his life.

Another formidable diplomat with whom I crossed paths was Ralph Bunche, in 1956. This was a man whose grandmother was born into slavery and achieved unimaginable success for the time. He was an American political scientist and diplomat who received the 1950 Nobel Peace Prize and had a long and distinguished career in international relations.

I met him when he traveled with his wife, and then again when he would stop over in Rome on his way to the Middle East. From the end of World War II, he became associated with the United Nations practically until he died, having been named acting U.N. mediator on Palestine. He did such a good job obtaining armistice agreements between Israel and the Arab states that upon returning home he received a hero's welcome and the Nobel Prize.

So I was overcome when he asked if I would accompany him to Via Veneto, so that we could sit in the open-air cafés and watch the celebrities parade up and down. Ralph Bunche did so enjoy this break in his busy schedule, and he didn't hesitate to bring me up-to-date on his family tragedies, either, including the suicide of his troubled daughter, who looked Caucasian but would have been classified as "black."

Some years ago, in the mid-1990s, when I became involved in the culinary activities of Villa d'Este, I accompanied Luciano Parolari, the executive chef, who was invited to the United Nations to prepare a gala dinner for Kofi Annan. I was speaking to some of the U.N. employees, and I asked them about Ralph Bunche, but none seemed to recognize his name. However, the next day Joan Bunche, another of his daughters, came and we lunched together. I was so proud of the fact that this incredible gentleman, one of the great minds of his time, should have honored me with his friendship. I shall never forget him.

Besides having the opportunity to rub shoulders with international figures, during my twenty years at TWA I was also wonderfully educated in the world of literature. This was the result of the visits of important journalists like Walter Lippmann, Art Buchwald, Herb Caen, Stan Delaplane, and Walter Cronkite and authors such as Vladimir Nabokov, Robert Ruark, Joseph Alsop, Joseph Heller, Irwin Shaw, John le Carré, and Bob Considine.

When any one of these writers was going to visit and needed to be met, escorted, or accompanied to social events, I would read about them and read their books and columns, in an effort to carry on an intelligent conversation when in their company. To me, this was what public relations was all about. It is also how I made friendships that have lasted a lifetime. I have always looked forward to meeting members of the press, especially writers. It is probably because I wanted to become one myself.

One of my favorites among the journalists was the travel writer Stan Delaplane. Stan wrote a travel column for the *San Francisco Chronicle,* and I love San Francisco!

There is something about San Francisco that I can't explain. Of course, New York is the city I love most because it is stimulating and I come alive there, but San Francisco is a city that makes me feel at home. It is the place where I had many friends, and that is what it is all about. I most prefer to travel to where I have friends.

Stan's column was syndicated in more than one hundred papers throughout the United States and Mexico. The first time I met him was during the 1950 Holy Year.

Stan came with a press group from the United States. This was the very first overseas flight non-stop from New York to Rome, and it created a lot of excitement. There was a fabulous program with visits to the head of state, Pope Pius XII, and the mayor of Rome. In the midst of all the running around, Stan Delaplane developed a toothache and was in such pain that I rushed him to my dentist, Pio Lalli.

When Stan discovered that Dr. Lalli had been Mussolini's dentist, he perked up because he had a "story." He nearly forgot about his tooth!

Stan received the Pulitzer Prize in 1942 for a story he wrote. He wrote for the *San Francisco Chronicle* for more than fifty-three years. The Washington Square Bar and Grill was where he would write his column while smoking and sipping a martini, his favorite drink.

Now that I am in my eighties, I do not think of myself as a full-fledged writer, but as a good reporter—otherwise how could I have put together my memoirs? Yes, it is all chronicled in my mind.

Of course, when I started my schooling in England, I was taught to keep a diary, and I've tried to update it, but I've had to rely on my memory to remember certain episodes.

Strolling through my diary has allowed me to visualize a long, otherwise forgotten lunch in Piazza Navona at the restaurant Tre Scalini, famous for its ice cream, which took place in 1958 with Art Buchwald, the syndicated columnist of the *International Her-ald Tribune,* the author Irwin Shaw, and my good friend David "Chim" Seymour.

The occasion was to celebrate the big success of Shaw's *The Young Lions*. The book had already been well received, but when it was turned into a movie starring Marlon Brando, it hit the jackpot. We were all feeling good, and Irwin Shaw was in great form because he was wearing the most elegant gabardine suit, made to order by Brioni, the number one tailor in Rome. We had made our selections from the menu, and we were enjoying some of the specialties when, all of a sudden, the lapels of Shaw's suit were spattered with olive oil, which spread all over.

Disaster! Shaw accused his table companions of not knowing how to eat properly, and he insisted that when seasoning the salad, Buchwald had squirted the oil all over.

We screamed at each other until we started roaring with laughter. What a riot!

On a more somber note, I shall never forget how much I enjoyed talking to the Lippmanns, for example. Helen, Walter's wife, was fluent in Italian because she had attended finishing schools in Florence. Walter Lippmannn, the influential award-winning writer, journalist, and political commentator who was the recipient of the Pulitzer Prize for his syndicated newspaper column, "Today and Tomorrow," visited Rome at least once a year, and my Luca would help him set up appointments with the Italian prime minister of the moment.

I also remember very well the very first time I met Robert Ruark, because I was nine months pregnant with my son, Andrea (only in those days we did not know the gender in advance). Today, more than forty years after his death, Ruark is almost forgotten, but in 1952, when we first met, he was arguably the most prolific and most popular writer in America. I was quite excited at the prospect of encountering him in person. I met him on the ramp as he deplaned, and I recognized him immediately, having seen his photo many times. I ran through my little spiel, which I ended by saying, "Is there anything I can do for you?" Ruark responded by going into his TWA overnight bag, fishing out a flask, quickly gulping down the liquor, and taking me under his arm.

"Do you have a car?"

"Yes," I replied.

"Okay," he said. "Let's go to the nearest hospital before you drop the baby on the ramp."

Of course Andrea took his time to make his entry into this world and didn't arrive until some days later.

Ruark stayed on in Rome and visited me with his wife, Virginia. When I returned home from the hospital, there were six dozen red roses waiting. I burst into tears and when I saw Robert I scolded him. I could have bought enough food to last a whole month for the price of those roses.

Ruark was so crazy about my son, "the drunken Irish man," as he called him, that he asked if he could adopt him, because he never had any children of his own.

"Absolutely not!" I said. "It took me nine months to produce this masterpiece."

Ruark was on the cover of *Time* magazine in the 1950s, and in his interview, he admitted that he spent a fortune on "booze." We continued to be fast friends until he died from the results of alcoholism in 1965.

Leo Rosten, otherwise known as Leonard Q. Ross, was one of the most interesting people I ever met, writer or not. I remember that he was an adviser to President Franklin Delano Roosevelt and he was a teacher and an academic. However, he was also a script writer and a humorist and he wrote a book, under the Ross pseudonym, that I think every American should read: *The Education of H*Y*M*A*N K*A*P*L*A*N.* It was first published in *The New Yorker* magazine in the 1930s. The book is hilarious. Another of his books that I continue to enjoy is *The Joys of Yiddish.*

I was working for TWA and first met him when I was sent to the airport for a celebrity greeting and we hit it off. In fact, one of his daughters, Peggy, spent a summer with us at our villa at Fregene.

I always think of Leo when I wear high heels. In the late 1950s it was very fashionable to wear spike-heeled shoes, but if I wore them, Leo was in a state of constant anxiety that I would fall. He worried so that he actually went to a store and bought me some flat-heeled shoes so I would be safe. The problem was that they resembled tennis shoes, so wearing them, especially at that time, when women never appeared on the street in "sneakers," was out of the question.

Another great literary friendship started during these years was with Joseph Heller of *Catch-22* fame. Heller is widely regarded as one of the best post-World War II satirists. He was as witty in person as he was in print, and he generously wrote the foreword to my book, *Villa d'Este Style,* in 2000. It turned out to be the last piece he wrote before his death later that year. I still miss him to this day; we were great friends and spent time together over many decades.

During this period I also developed my own literary prowess. In addition to my duties at TWA, in 1961 I had become a columnist for the insert of the Italian weekly *Amica,* the magazine of the Italian newspaper *Corriere della Sera,* one of the top, if not the number one, dailies. One particularly memorable event was my interview with Gloria Swanson. I treasure any advice that is given to me, especially when it comes from a source as reliable as Gloria. She was most prominent during the silent film era as both an actress and a fashion icon, although today she is best known for her role as Norma Desmond in the film *Sunset Boulevard,* and that is just when I meet her.

Gloria had just made a comeback with the film, also starring William Holden and Erich von Stroheim. She was staying at a friend's house in Rome and she went out of her way to help me with the interview. She was so eager to show me how I should dress, how I should walk, how I should do my hair—that she put me in front of a tall looking glass. She showed me how important it was to keep the proportions. It was like a finishing school.

Then she said, "Look at me, I am completely out of proportion, but I have learned to dress myself and nobody can tell." I treasured all her suggestions, and to this day I think of her when I am trying out some new fashion or outfit.

The 1960s turned out to be the most entertaining years. I met so many wonderful people and I learned something from each one. Even from Queen Elizabeth.

Because I had become a gossip columnist for *Amica,* I was invited to all the major social events in Rome, including a soirée at the Quirinale, the Italian version of Buckingham Palace, in honor of a visit by Queen Elizabeth and Prince Philip.

I was so excited because I've always admired Elizabeth, who, like me, was born under the sign of Taurus; we are the same age, only a few days apart. For the occasion I decided to have a new dress made by my seamstress. I bought a green taffeta brocade fabric with a Scottish plaid design. Naturally it became a long evening dress, and it went well with my flaming red hair and freckles.

Finally the day arrived, and we got in line to enter. The royal guests were all arranged, the ladies in the front row and the gentlemen in the back. Once we had settled in the immense salon, the queen, followed by the prince, made her entrance, and I was quite surprised to see how tiny she was . . . but ever so regal. Prince Philip dropped a few steps behind the queen and stopped to talk to me!

He asked if I was Scottish and was surprised when I said I was Italian. I don't remember what else he asked me; I was quite embarrassed that I had caught his attention.

When we returned home my husband said, "Now I know why you went to all that trouble. You were hoping to catch the prince's attention."

Of course he was right—but I never thought it would happen.

While we are on the subject of royalty, King Michael of Romania, better known as the King of the Romanians, was the last monarch behind the Iron Curtain to lose his throne. He is a cousin of Queen Elizabeth, and in 1947 he attended her wedding to Prince Philip. On this occasion he met Princess Anne of Bourbon-Parma, and in 1948 they got married. They had five daughters and they lived most of their lives in exile.

I went to meet them at the airport and, as usual, the flight was late. The wait was worthwhile, though, because they were utterly charming. There is a photograph of our meeting and you can see in the background the police and the airport employees—stretching their necks, hoping to get into the picture.

Ironically, I was "touched" by the royals on one other occasion, through my dear friend Irving Hoffman, the columnist and publicist. As I waded through stacks of photos showing my grandparents, my parents, and more recent family, friends, and celebrities that I wanted to remember in this book, I thought I had mentioned all those who left a mark on me—and then I suddenly came across a batch of letters from my pal Irving Hoffman, who died in 1968 at the age of fifty-nine.

Irving was a caricaturist, and I have over the years collected quite a few of his drawings. One I especially treasure is what Irving drew as the cover for the book he wanted me to write, which he called *Roll Out the Red Carpet.* Incredibly, he suggested it during my years at TWA. I met him first in the early 1950s, and he proved to be one of the best friends one could ever dream of having.

Hoffman was known mainly for his column "Tales of Hoffman," appearing in *The Hollywood Reporter,* and he was, of course, widely read and known. He was an intimate of Irving Berlin—who "tested" new songs on him. Judy Garland, Shirley McLaine, and Lauren Bacall were fortunate to be assisted by him in his role as press agent, because he certainly helped them in their careers. He was blind as a bat, but as he said, he "got by."

Hoffman's wit gave him access to the crème de la crème and their parties. On occasion, he would upset the status quo by selling gossip to his friends (and roommates at 156 West 48th Street in Manhattan) Damon Runyon, Walter Winchell, and Ed Sullivan. But his biggest career coup involved the King and Queen of England and some hotdogs. It took place in 1939.

One of his promotions was as press agent for the amusement park, Coney Island, in New York City. King George VI and Queen Elizabeth of England were visiting the U.S. as the guests of Franklin D. Roosevelt. Roosevelt took the royals on a trip to Coney Island, where Hoffman, brilliantly, arranged to have them photographed eating a Nathan's hotdog. The picture ran throughout the world, resulting in free publicity for the beach community, for Nathan's, and for hotdogs in general.

Hoffman also made some journalistic scoops when he printed the personal comments of Adolf Hitler on various American movies. Because I met so many interesting people, Irving wanted me to write about them. He went so far as to have Helen Strauss, the creator of the literary department at the William Morris Agency and probably the most powerful literary agent of her time, make a trip to Rome to see me during the early 1960s to discuss the possibility of my book. It didn't work out. I was scared stiff of her.

Time went by, and Irving and I kept up our daily correspondence until 1968, when I realized that Irving was very ill. I took a plane and went to New York. I was allowed to visit, but I was not to let anybody know that I had seen him. When I arrived, he was propped up in a wheelchair and assisted by two nurses. I had to fight back the tears because it was quite obvious that he was on his way "out."

Irving was still living on West 48th Street, and when I left the apartment I walked for hours, crying and sobbing. So it is thanks to my dear friend Irving Hoffman that I have written this memoir. It just took me fifty years to take his advice!

Every day I would check with TWA reservations to see if there was any VIP arriving or departing about whom I should make a fuss, and it was through the daily check that I discovered that the writer William Faulkner, winner of the Nobel Prize in Literature in 1949, was booked to leave Rome for New York.

On the spur of the moment, I looked up his local contact and called. Having explained who I was, I told him that we had reserved a nice seat for him, but we needed to know whether he preferred an aisle or a window. If I remember correctly, he said aisle; I said that I would come to the hotel to see him off.

When I arrived, he said, "Why don't you come out to the airport with me?" (I assumed he was one of the many who didn't enjoy flying). I gladly accepted, and we had a most enjoyable drive and I discovered a little bit about his thoughts on a number of issues.

For example, at some point Faulkner announced that everyone referred to the United States as a "melting pot," and it would not be long before we would be able to visualize the term because all Americans would be a "caffé latte" color. As I look around today, years later, I have to agree with William Faulkner because we are all turning the color of a "cappuccino."

But back to *Amica,* where I scored another great interview for the magazine provided by the arrival of Danny Kaye and his wife, Sylvia Fine. Their flight had arrived late, and it was pitch dark as they emerged from the plane.

The passengers looked worn and bedraggled, especially one mother with a screaming baby in her arms.

It didn't take Danny Kaye long to improvise an act to humor the child, who ended up in *his* arms. Actually, the whole planeload of passengers enjoyed the show that he put on. No wonder he was appointed ambassador-at-large for the United Nations Children's Emergency Fund.

Danny Kaye performed on the stage in the movies, in nightclubs, and in vaudeville. He received many decorations and he was honored by the French government as an officer of the Ordre des Arts et des Lettres (only Charlie Chaplin before him had been presented with this order).

Danny Kaye came also to Villa d'Este during my tenure there as PR director and that is when I found out that he loved to cook, so we treated him to a visit to the kitchen to meet our chef.

Apart from Marcello Mastroianni, who was probably better known abroad than in Italy, there was handsome Vittorio Gassman, a great Shakespearean actor, a comedian, and very popular in the legitimate theater. He was married at one time to actress Shelley Winters, the "dumb blonde" who became a serious stage and film actress.

Also near the top of the list of great Latin lovers is Walter Chiari. He had a much-publicized romance with the most beautiful woman in the world, Ava Gardner, whose marriage to Frank Sinatra had broken up. Ava and Sinatra had spent their honeymoon at Villa d'Este. Chiari followed Ava to Australia and back, but this stormy romance also came to an abrupt end. Ava Gardner really didn't care about making a career in the movies. Instead her name was linked with bullfighters, actors, writers, and the list grows.

We don't know whether it was due to Ava Gardner that Walter Chiari became a star overnight and was offered the leading role in a Broadway show titled *The Gay Life*. I wonder what the play would be titled today! It lasted six months on Broadway.

In 1962 I was to interview Alberto Moravia, the novelist. He was quite renowned at the time and so I was incredibly nervous. Moravia was born in 1907, the child of a wealthy family, and raised at home because of illness. He published his first novel, *The Time of Indifference*, at the age of twenty-three. Banned from publishing under Mussolini, he emerged after World War II as one of the most admired and influential twentieth-century Italian writers.

When I called Moravia, he gave me an appointment in his apartment overlooking the Piazza del Popolo and the famous Caffé Rosati, which had become a meeting place for the intelligentsia known as the "liberals."

Luca accompanied me and waited at the Caffé Rosati. I forgot to mention that my Luca was frightfully jealous and this also made me very nervous. Moravia was known to be quite a man about town, and his estranged wife Elsa Morante lived in the same building as her ex-husband. Together they were considered the top authors, not just in Italy but also in all of Europe.

Moravia, whose real name was Pincherle, had to go into hiding when the Germans occupied Rome because his family was Jewish. Fortunately Mussolini's son-in-law Galeazzo Ciano protected him, and that is how he survived.

Finally I was in the presence of Moravia, and suddenly I was so intimidated and overwhelmed in the presence of such literary royalty, albeit "out of office" royalty, that I was unable to speak and I felt like an utter fool! How was this possible? I have rarely been tongue-tied in my life.

Moravia was becoming quite impatient, but he must have felt sorry for me. I showed him the questions that I had typed and was planning to ask him, and he took the sheet, sat at his desk, and started typing the answers. When he was through, knowing that I had a photographer with me, he invited me to step out on the terrace, and we had our photo taken.

I swore the photographer to secrecy about my incompetence. I was so ashamed to admit that I couldn't conduct the interview. I confided in Oriana Fallaci, who tried to convince me to stick to it and persevere in my career as an interviewer, but I preferred to quit. This made Luca very happy.

In 1960 the Olympic Games took place in Rome. This was the most exciting event since the end of World War II, bar none. I had to take advantage and figure out a way to get TWA into the press "picture."

I set out for the Olympic Village, which was on a site along the ancient Via Flaminia. This area along the flood plain of the Tiber had historically been used as a site for sporting events. It was easily accessible to Foro Italico across the river, which already had a stadium, and there was also a existing hippodrome on the site of the village. Two new stadiums had been built, housing for the athletes was complete, and an entire community had been created that included shopping, schools, and a church.

I was accompanied on my expedition by a photographer and the best-looking TWA hostess I could find. Once at the village, I managed to obtain a permit and we roamed around, taking photos at random of the various athletes, always making sure the shot included the TWA hostess at the side of the athlete.

I was rather embarrassed because I didn't recognize any of the athletes, but I ran into a very nice-looking African-American man who let me take his photo. He seemed very sympathetic, so I decided to confide in him. I confessed that I didn't know anybody at the village—athletes or personnel—and wondered how I would be able to caption the photographs.

My newly acquired friend offered, "I'll help you." He seemed to know everybody! I asked his name. "Jesse Owens," he said.

I collected my photographer and my hostess and my captions, thanked Jesse Owens, and went back to the office.

Naturally I told everyone how lucky I was to have met this terrific guy named Jesse Owens who had helped me out. My colleagues were astonished. How could I not have known who Jesse Owens was? He was one of the greatest athletes of all time, the greatest track star ever, and hero of the 1936 Olympics in Berlin. He had won four gold medals, providing a huge source of embarrassment to the Nazi exponents of Aryan supremacy and a huge source of pride to the Americans.

When Donna de Varona, the former world-class swimmer, visited Villa d'Este in 2009, I told her my story about Jesse Owens and how embarrassed I had been that I did not recognize him. Then Donna told me something: At age 13, she had been the youngest swimmer to compete at the 1960 Summer Olympics. In her career, Donna told me, she set eighteen swimming records. After the 1964 Olympics she retired and signed a contract with ABC, becoming the first female sportscaster in television history.

But now back to the 1960s. It was the summer of 1963 when I got the call from Letitia Baldridge, former assistant to Clare Boothe Luce, the U.S. ambassador to Italy. In later years, Tish served as social secretary and chief of staff to Jacqueline Kennedy.

She was traveling with Jacqueline Kennedy via TWA on their way to Greece. The flight was making a forty-five-minute stopover at Rome's

Fiumicino Airport, but Mrs. Kennedy did not want the U.S. embassy to get involved, so I was not to let anyone know that she was at the Rome airport. This was a private trip; Mrs. Kennedy was mourning her son Patrick Bouvier Kennedy, who had died a few days after birth. Tish Baldridge asked me to meet their flight and make sure that nobody would try to go near Mrs. Kennedy. This was quite understandable; after all she had been through.

When the flight arrived, I met the ladies outside on the ramp. They were the last to disembark. Tish introduced me, and I said the most obvious thing that came to mind: "How was the flight?"

Without looking at me, and staring into space, Mrs. Kennedy whispered, "Delicious."

That was the extent of our conversation. My heart went out to her because losing a child, in my mind, is the worst tragedy a mother can suffer. And I heard after the fact that she was very grateful that she had not been bothered during the stopover. It was an exciting moment for me, even though the circumstances were laden with sadness, to meet the First Lady who, at that time, was already an international icon. And, of course, this was not the last horrific tragedy she would suffer in her lifetime. It was inconceivable at the time that her husband would soon be assassinated and her life would change permanently.

Also in 1963, the Hilton Hotel in Rome was about to be inaugurated and, according to tradition, Conrad Hilton himself would open the doors. By that time, my husband, Luca, had left TWA and was now the head of sales for the soon-to-open Hilton, located on the dramatic hilltop of Monte Mario, overlooking the city of Rome. The launch of this major new hotel in Rome was to be quite a spectacular event.

Already the hotel was filled with press who had come from all parts of the world to write about the experience. It's important to stress again that at this time, Rome was the center of the world in terms of entertainment—with American movies being made here, and stars galore—so it was glamour central, and the press relished an opportunity to visit and write about what was happening in Rome.

The columnist Bob Considine, who was a good friend of ours and a very eclectic writer—first of novels and screenplays, and later as a Hearst columnist—was scheduled to cover the opening ceremony.

According to *Time* magazine, "Bob Considine is . . . the Hearstling who regularly gets there first with the most words on almost any subject." Unfortunately for the press covering the hotel inauguration, Pope John XXIII died suddenly, postponing the original launch date and creating something of a frenzy as reporters having been called to cover the launch sat with nothing to report.

This meant that Bob Considine would stay over until the new pope was elected, and this is where my Luca came to his aid, giving him the chance to scoop all the other journalists. First he put a TV set in Bob's room so that Bob would have up-to-the-minute information and know immediately when the announcement of the election of the new pope was made; and second, Luca installed an open telephone line to New York. This was critical—it was open only to Bob, and it gave him unique and fast access to his home office.

So Considine got the scoop. He was the first in the world to report the election of the new pope, Paul VI on June 21, 1963. I happened to be at the airport, seeing VIPs off, and Luca called with the news. I grabbed the loudspeaker and made the announcement to the public at large. While I was broadcasting the news at the airport, Bob Considine was broadcasting his appreciation for TWA and the Hilton Hotel's assistance in securing this scoop for years to come.

Once it was inaugurated, the Hilton was the venue for the best events. It was the iconic venue of *La Dolce Vita* and therefore we decided to hold my daughter Claudia's first Holy Communion reception there in 1964. Luca secured the hotel; my role was to dress Claudia for the occasion. In Italy, the girls are always dressed like bridesmaids in organdy and taffeta. Instead of following this tradition, I designed a very plain white cotton piqué sheath, which really made her stand out because of its monastic simplicity. I thought she looked utterly precious. Some forty years later I was cleaning out a closet and I found Claudia's dress for her first communion, so I asked if she cared to keep it.

"Definitely no!" she said. "You might as well know that I hated you for dressing me like a poor nun, while all the other girls were dressed to the nines. I felt like Little Orphan Annie at my communion!"

So much for my attempt at distinction!

But now back to the writers of the era and here I have to include Oriana Fallaci, the Italian journalist, author, and interviewer, who was not only a colleague, but also a friend.

The year was 1956 when Oriana asked me if I would accompany her to New York. She wanted my help in getting an interview with Marilyn Monroe. Oriana knew that, thanks to TWA, I had made some very good contacts, especially in the entertainment field and because, at the time, she couldn't speak any English, she needed me as her interpreter.

Oriana and I walked everywhere, like all tourists who arrive in New York for the first time. Actually, I had already made a few trips (three, to be exact) to the United States from the time I was hired in Rome. I felt very pleased with myself because I was in a position where I could show my friends around Manhattan, acting as a guide.

The more I think about Oriana, the more I miss her—she was always on the lookout for me. The Oriana I knew was thoughtful and kind at all times. Well, back to our adventure in New York City.

The two of us set out, and upon arriving in New York I started making calls. On the top of my call list was Irving Hoffman, because Irving knew everybody. I was sure that he would know how to get in touch with M.M.

We soon found out that M.M. was in hiding. Later we learned that Milton H. Greene, her agent, was getting ready to announce that she was about to marry Arthur Miller. It was the best-kept secret of the time.

When Irving admitted that he had to give up because there was no available access, I thought I would try calling some of my columnist friends, Leonard Lyons, Louis Sobol, even Louella Parsons and Hedda Hopper. Of course, this was absurdly naive of me because even if they knew where and why she was hiding, they were not about to tell me. This had to be the scoop of the year.

Oriana and I became the talk of the town during this visit. We were mentioned in all the columns as "two girls from Rome" (Oriana was actually a true Florentine and very proud of it), who were "in New York hoping to bump into M.M.!"

We received some phony calls from people who gave us indications as to where we might find M.M. One night we were in a theater where we were assured that the star of the moment would show up, maybe in disguise or wearing a black wig. We took all suggestions into consideration and attended the play, *Joan of Arc* starring Julie Harris. We kept scanning the audience, and especially during the intermissions we looked high and low for Marilyn.

The play ended and we looked around, but did not see anybody who could resemble the divine Marilyn. Then we had a bright idea. Surely Marilyn would have wanted to congratulate Julie Harris on her performance! So we proceeded to the backstage dressing rooms, where we were sure we would find her.

But we were out of luck because the lights had been turned out and we had to make our way back into the theater. Even here it was pitch dark, but somehow we made our way to the exit—only to realize that we had been locked in. At this point we had exhausted ourselves. Clearly there was no way out. We decided to go to sleep in the front row seats.

About four a.m., the night watchman woke us up. This was the last straw! We needed our rest!

Our names appeared in the columns of Louis Sobol and Leonard Lyons the next day, and Oriana and I became the laughingstocks of New York. Word reached Luca, who threatened to divorce me if I didn't return *tout de suite!* Oriana didn't want to leave New York, but without my assistance as her interpreter, she had no choice. So the two of us very forlornly and in a weepy mood boarded our flight home. We discussed at length how best to remedy such a waste of our time chasing M.M. in vain.

And then we had a brainstorm: How about writing a story about how we did *not* get to interview Marilyn Monroe? Oriana liked the idea and got carried away. She wrote a great article about our New York adventures, and as a result Angelo Rizzoli, the Italian publisher and film producer, sent her roses, praised her, and hired her. Oriana's book, *I Sette Peccati di Hollywood (The Seven Sins of Hollywood),* with a preface by Orson Welles, was published in 1958 in Italy by Longanesi/Rizzoli (but never translated into English). It was a big success.

Here is Oriana's rendition of the story, from that book.

We arrived in New York on Thursday, in the morning. The following evening we still had no indication on how to get in touch with Marilyn, even though all our Italian colleagues were participating in our efforts. One was going to the theater, one to the cinema, one to the restaurant she usually patronized. In two evenings we visited twelve restaurants, eighteen nightclubs, eight cinemas, fourteen theaters.

Jean Govoni Salvadore, a Roman friend who had many important friends in New York, was going out of her mind. After all the vain searches, her delicate white face, framed by fiery red hair, looked like she was ill—but I was sure we would succeed. Jean thought of phoning Irving Hoffman: He was one of the publicity men best known in the States and he was the one who gave me fifteen minutes of unexpected publicity. It was Irving Hoffman who escorted the Queen Mother to eat hot dogs in a drugstore when, not yet crowned, she went to the States with Philip. Hoffman was very close to Marilyn, who once declared, "I would do anything for Irving Hoffman."

We asked his help with the same tone of voice you would use to call a doctor in the middle of the night.

"Very simple," said Irving. "I even have her home address: 60 Sutton Place. I will send her a telegram right now."

That evening we ate with appetite and went to bed without visits, not even to the nightclub. We fell asleep dreaming of Irving Hoffman. But the next day he called and his voice was very sad: The address was wrong. Marilyn had left that apartment one month before.

We were informed that Steven Kaufmann, one of the wealthiest men in New York and a great fan of Marilyn, was probably aware of her new address.

When we met him, Steven Kaufmann offered a shot of whisky and said, "Please, now relax," and he suggested that we get in touch with Leonard Lyons. We called Leonard, and his wife, Sylvia, told us that he had left for Moscow and suggested we call Earl Blackwell, known as Mr. Celebrity, because he had the address of all celebrities. We called him in Chicago, but, regretfully, the address of Marilyn was the only one he did not have at hand.

By that time, all New York was aware of the fact that an Italian journalist was trying to interview Marilyn Monroe, without success.

A few days later, journalists started calling me because they wanted an interview. They were asking for my curriculum vitae, wanted to take a picture, and were interested in whatever I was doing. When Jean and I, by mistake, were closed inside a theatre on 48th Street and were obliged to sleep for the entire night on the chairs in the pit, the columnist Louis Sobol wrote about the incident.

It is very easy in the States to gain a moment of celebrity. Jean and I had our moment, but we were terrified.

Louella Parsons called from Hollywood. Jean had a headache and I had stomach trouble. We were unable to go to a cocktail party because we were immediately recognized, surrounded, and examined. Everybody was making a bet: "Will the Italian journalist be able to interview Monroe?" Many were positive; others were of the opinion that Milton Greene would never allow it. "He has hypnotized her, do you understand? He is hiding her and doing whatever he wants with her to make her more interesting. You do understand that that poor girl is like the Bank of England?" they all asked.

Tuesday afternoon, when my flight was booked, and we departed New York, it was like a gift from God for me; while Jean, instead, was so sad to leave.

Back in Milan I wrote an article that paid me double of what I had earned on any earlier article. Some of the readers sent me bunches of roses, to make up for what I had suffered, while others sent me letters of sympathy. For a couple of months Irving Hoffman sent me newspaper clippings with mentions of my name, but only one of them had my name spelled correctly—the one written by Igor Cassini, who had dedicated half of his article to King Baldovino and the other half to me. It ended with "Marilyn, how precious you are!"

I stuck it on the wall of the editing office, to keep my pride in check.

From that day forward, Oriana was under contract to Rizzoli for every book she wrote until her dying day.

Oriana was based in Milan, while I was in Rome, but we still managed to get together. She was a good friend, and when I started writing my column in *Amica* in 1961 she sent me a letter, which I have always kept, just after she had read my first article. Naturally the letter is in Italian, but here it is translated.

Dear Jean,

In the midst of a nervous breakdown, which I am taking care of, but only for a few days, here in Florence, I remembered (or was it a dream?) that one day, one morning I think, you called my house and you said that you would call back. Instead you never called.

I repeat, maybe I dreamed it all but, if it happened, you made a big mistake in not calling me back. Stop.

Anyway this letter is not to scold you, it is to congratulate you.

I bought, notwithstanding my utter dislike, a copy of Corriere della Sera, Amica, *and the only good thing inside, I mean the only thing, is your column, which is not good: It is very, very good. Interesting, amusing, vivacious, intelligent, well written.*

Also, Govoni in the photograph is pretty with all her big teeth.

As usual, though, the Italians are full of shit, and they are always afraid to publicize the others. Why didn't they explain, in a brief biographical note, who you are and why you know all those fools? I, who know that you really do know them, I believe and I rejoice. Only a few others who know you also believe you. But the majority of the readers ignore it and are authorized to suspect a trick; all the more because your name in the world of journalism is new and it doesn't show anywhere that you have interviewed those fools or whatever.

Therefore if the editors of the newspaper were not so afraid of giving you publicity they should have said, for example, "Giovanna Govoni, who knows everybody," or else you should do it in one of the openings of your column. This way it would result more lively and sharp.

Lots of kisses and once again brava,
Oriana

P.S. Let them put a bigger photo and all the rest.

My trip with Oriana was only one of so many trips to New York. In my position I enjoyed several privileges, such as a pass valid for all TWA destinations. So there were many occasions when I would board a plane on the spur of the moment and fly to New York.

Yes, New York is my favorite city in the whole world. This is where I have the most friends and where I might take up residence when I retire—which I am still not quite ready to do, notwithstanding the fact that I'm decades beyond a normal retirement age at this point in my life, being in my eighties.

But I must go off on a tangent or two before I get back to the topic of Oriana and me.

I met Shirley MacLaine through Oriana Fallaci. Shirley, the singer, actress, dancer, writer, and spiritual crusader, had never before visited Rome, so Oriana asked me to look after her when she visited in 1961. I went to meet Shirley upon arrival at the airport, all dressed up in my new "Chanel" suit, which my seamstress had just delivered. It was a brilliant copy; it looked like the real McCoy!

The plane arrived on time and I met Shirley at the bottom of the steps. I had no problem recognizing her, but I was taken aback when I realized that she was wearing the same Chanel suit that I had on— the only difference was that Shirley's outfit was authentic and mine was a copy!

In 1962 I decided to spend a weekend in New York visiting with friends. I had not been able to find the time to write and my correspondence was piling up. I could not write to everybody, so I thought that if I showed up in person it would be appreciated.

In 1962 Rome was buzzing with excitement. Twentieth Century Fox was filming *Cleopatra* on location in Italy. The star was Elizabeth Taylor, who, together with Richard Burton (and Rex Harrison) almost managed to put the production out of business, their fees were so expensive. It was rumored that Taylor and Burton had a budding romance, which kept the paparazzi on the run.

Taylor and Burton did not seem to mind—sometimes I thought that they intentionally encouraged the press to catch up with them! Who knows?

Anyway, I arrived at the airport and the big excitement was that Burton was there and was about to board my flight to New York. His press agent saw me and rushed over, asking me to take care of Burton, who was disembarking in Paris; the flight was making an interim stop there. Burton was doing a one-day stint in the movie *The Longest Day*, so he needed to be there for a short time only. All the major actors in that film had cameo roles, each of which consisted of a one-day shoot. I was introduced to Burton, and he immediately took me under his arm, cuddled up, and whispered, "Let's give the press something to write about and let's make Elizabeth jealous."

The plane took off, and while Burton stopped in Paris I remained on board because the French press had gathered around the bottom of the steps waiting for me to appear. Word got around that I was Burton's new conquest! When I arrived in New York, all hell broke loose. I never saw such a turnout, and I couldn't believe that they were there for me. As I deplaned, I was unrecognizable; even my PR colleagues who were waiting for me didn't know who I was. I had a scarf around my head, tied up à la Queen Elizabeth so my red hair was invisible (it was always a real giveaway as to my identity), and I wore dark glasses. I looked like someone who really wanted to be recognized but was pretending to travel incognito.

Finally, and only with the assistance of the TWA staff, I was shoved into a limousine—but one guy managed to break through the crowd and yell, "If you let me interview you I'll give you five hundred dollars!" Finally I was on my way to Manhattan and feeling somewhat relieved when panic again set in. I suddenly realized that my gorgeous husband was a very jealous Sicilian and he would certainly be aware of my escapade. I called him as soon as I arrived at my hotel and, sure enough, he was fuming.

"What are you up to?" he demanded. Naturally I got on the first plane available and returned to my one and only, who didn't think it was so funny to have his wife's photo published in all the gossip columns on both sides of the Atlantic. In the end the press realized that Burton loved practical jokes, so the whole story was quickly forgotten.

A few weeks later I received a call from my friends at Twentieth Century Fox, again asking for my help. Eddie Fisher was on his way to Rome. In 1959, Eddie had been married to Debbie Reynolds (they were known as "America's sweethearts"), and he had divorced Debbie so that he could marry Elizabeth, who had been widowed by Mike Todd's death. Now Eddie kept hearing rumors that his wife and Burton were possibly having an affair, so he decided to look into the matter and flew to Rome via TWA to see for himself. I was the only one on hand to meet him, no Elizabeth! I was so embarrassed, particularly when he asked me what the status of the Richard-Elizabeth relationship was. I told him that all I knew was what I read in the papers.

We all know how the story ended. After Eddie and Elizabeth divorced, Burton became Elizabeth's fifth husband, and later her sixth.

I remember the first time I met "La Liz," I was working for TWA and she arrived on her honeymoon with Nicky Hilton. I went to greet them with Luca, who pushed me aside and said, "I'll take care of this arrival." All she had to do was bat her beautiful violet eyes and my Luca nearly fainted.

When I joined Villa d'Este in 1967, I met the concierge, Carlo Magni, who had been with the hotel for fifty years. He was very discreet and he had turned down an offer to write about the famous guests he had known and observed. He would share only the harmless anecdotes. Known as "the concierge of the iron gate," he told me that Elizabeth Taylor still owed him three mystery books that she borrowed during her honeymoon stay with Nicky Hilton at the Villa d'Este in 1950. It appears that marriage was rocky from the start if midnight reading was a mainstay of the honeymoon.

As it turns out, I came to discover that Elizabeth and I grew up in the same neighborhood in London.

In the 1930s, when my family lived in Golders Green, a section of London, I attended school at a convent called La Sagesse Convent. It was here that I met Elizabeth Bogarde, who was to become my best friend, and her brother, Dirk, who also became my friend, and a famous actor, too. Their parents met mine and so we all became the best of friends, even after my family left London to travel to Paris, and ultimately back to Italy when the war began.

During the early 1950s, I asked Luca to take me to London, because I was trying "to explore my roots." He reluctantly agreed, and I was ever so excited because I wanted to catch up with the Bogardes, visit Golders Green and La Sagesse Convent, and see the house where I had lived with my family.

Luca and I were staying at the Savoy Hotel in London, so one morning I asked the concierge to reserve a car and driver to take us to Golders Green.

The concierge gave me a surprised look when I made this request and made it clear he didn't think it was such a good idea to visit Golders Green, but he didn't explain why. So off we went to explore my past.

We arrived in Golders Green and I helped the driver find Ambrose Avenue, the street where we had lived. We drove along until I recognized my house, and then I understood why the concierge, and probably the driver too, were shocked that I had come from Italy to visit this very rundown neighborhood.

I had told friends and acquaintances that I had grown up in an English villa. Clearly my memory had forsaken me. Shocked by what

I was seeing as opposed to my memory, I did not even get out of the car and, pretending nothing was unusual, I asked the driver to follow my instructions and take me to my school, La Sagesse Convent. I remembered how to get there because as a child I had walked to school each day.

When we arrived at the gates of the convent, which I recognized immediately, there was a big sign that read Jewish Day Center. I was completely dumbfounded. Somehow La Sagesse Convent, known as a Catholic institution, had become a Jewish one. As I pondered how to proceed (should I go inside and try to find acquaintances?), I spotted a woman carrying two shopping bags from Sainsbury's market coming down the street. She dragged by and my driver called after her, "Excuse me, ma'am, for I 'ave a lady in the car who is looking for the school she went to before the war. She says it was called La Sagesse Convent."

With that the woman dropped her bags and exclaimed, "I don't believe it. That is where I went to school!"

I got out of the car and we embraced as if we had always known each other. This was an almost impossible coincidence and although I didn't recognize her, I was happy nonetheless to validate my memories of school and she helped me do that.

Later that day I called Dirk Bogarde to tell him about my discovery of the classmate and the changeover in institution. After all, he had attended the same school, and I thought he would be tickled pink to hear my story. I was mistaken.

He made me promise that I would never mention Golders Green again because it had become beyond less than chic. He suggested that if anyone answered where I had lived in London and attended school, I should answer Hampstead Heath.

Dirk explained that, although Elizabeth Taylor and Jean Simmons (and the two of us, of course) came from Golders Green, Dirk in his autobiographies, and Elizabeth Taylor in hers, too, always named their "hometown" as Hampstead Heath.

Okay, so back to Oriana.

"Oriana, did I ever tell you how I met Paul Newman?"

Oriana Fallaci and I were spending the evening together in my New York hotel the night before my TWA farewell party at 21 Club in June of 1966. The party was hosted by TWA and the owners of the 21 Club, the Kriendler family, including Pete and Jeannette, Bob and Florence, and Karen.

My departure was somewhat unexpected. I felt that I had it all: I had my glamorous job as head of PR for TWA, which allowed me a pass so I could travel anywhere around the world; my regular column in *Amica;* two wonderful kids; lots of interesting friends; an apartment in Rome with a villa in Fregene; and an adoring husband. What could be better?

Unfortunately, my adoring husband was restless, and that is why he accepted a job as public relations director for Angelo Rizzoli—unbeknownst to me. This would not have been a problem except that he would be relocated to Milan. That meant that I too, along with our family, would be relocated to Milan—something of an unexpected bump in my perfect life.

Thus my farewell party in 1966 at TWA, since there was no way for me to work at TWA and live in Milan. I was somewhat despondent; on the other hand, it was a new chapter, and I was excited at the prospects for the future. I was about to turn forty, something of a landmark age. Oriana and I discussed all of these subjects at great length that night.

Back to Paul Newman: I told Oriana that in 1962 *Amica* had wanted me to go to Hollywood for the Academy Awards. The 1962 awards were particularly important to Italians because the word was out that our Sophia Loren was going to win Best Actress for her role in the film *Two Women;* if she won, it would be the first time an Academy Award was given for a non-English-speaking performance. The film was scripted from the Alberto Moravia novel *La Ciociara* and directed by the great Vittorio De Sica; it tells the story of a woman trying to protect her teenage daughter from the horrors of the war.

When I spoke to Loren to announce that I was going to accompany her to Los Angeles, she said, "But I am not going!" She had decided that unless she was assured that she would win the Academy Award, she was not going to attend the ceremony. We all decided to attend without her—the producer, the director, and everybody around her—insisting that the Oscar would be hers and that by not attending, "You are not being a good sport."

I was going. I had friends in Hollywood like Army Archerd and Van Heflin, who were going to attend with me. I had a magazine that wanted me to write an article, and I had a yen to attend this event, which would be a first for me. So I booked myself on a TWA flight from Rome to New York and on to Los Angeles.

The day I checked in at the Rome Airport of Fiumicino, guess what? I bumped into Paul Newman and his wife, Joanne Woodward, who coincidentally were on their way to Los Angeles to attend the Academy Awards as Paul was nominated for Best Actor for *The Hustler.* (He sadly didn't win, but we didn't know that then. By the end of his career he had ten Academy Award nominations, but had won for Best Actor once, for *The Color of Money* in 1987, but also received an Honorary Academy Award in 1986 and the Jean Hersholt Humanitarian Award in 1994.)

But the fact that he had not yet won an Oscar did not deter my interest: It had to be my lucky day! I introduced myself and asked whether we could have a chat. He responded, "By all means. As soon as Joanne goes to sleep, let's sit up front and have a talk." At this time TWA was still running the Super Constellations, so it took at least twenty-four hours to fly to California; Paul Newman and I would have all the time in the world to get to know each other, and I was in seventh heaven.

Paul Newman certainly didn't behave like a movie star. He was so down-to-earth, I felt as if I had always known him. I was intrigued by the fact that he was knitting for most of the trip—not something I would have expected. He explained that his doctor had suggested it as a relaxation technique. He seemed to be quite accomplished in the knitting of a scarf.

At this point I must mention the Heflins, because I will always remember how they helped me out when I arrived in Los Angeles for the Academy Awards.

Growing up, Van Heflin was torn between becoming a sailor or an actor. He finally settled for the screen and the stage. On stage he had a part in *The Philadelphia Story* with Katharine Hepburn; in the 1940s he was a leading man in many successful movies. In the late 1940s I met him and his family in Rome. His wife, Frances Neal (sister of Pat Neal), and their children, Vana, Kate, and Tracy, became our friends.

When I arrived at the awards in 1962, the Heflins accompanied me to the theater, got me a seat, and introduced me around. Also joining our group was Army Archerd, whom I had met during my early TWA days. He was hired in 1953 by *Daily Variety* to replace Sheilah Graham. His column, "Just for Variety," became ever so popular, and it covered it all.

About our encounter at the Academy Awards, Army wrote that I had flown over for Sophia Loren, who didn't show up because she wasn't sure that she would get an Oscar. She did win, but what a shame that she did not pick it up in person and it was accepted, instead, by Greer Garson.

Part Three
The Villa d'Este Years
1966-Present

The year was 1966, and it provided an important turning point in my life and in the life of my family, too. We left our beloved Rome, the Fregene beach house, my glamorous job; my kids left their school, their friends, and the great weather to go . . . where? To Milan! We had to be crazy to abandon Rome, the most beautiful city in the world, to live instead in dreary Milan. We had everything going for us in Rome; it was too good to be true. But my Luca was restless. One day he came home and announced, "Start packing, we are going to move to Milan."

I was speechless. When I pulled myself together, I tried to find out more about this earth-shattering news. Luca didn't give me much satisfaction apart from the fact that I would have to quit my job with TWA because Luca's new boss, Angelo Rizzoli, the newspaper and book publishing magnate, did not want the wives of his editors to work; he worried that friends would think that he wasn't offering his associates adequate salaries if they had working wives.

Of course, being a dutiful Italian wife, I started packing and I didn't give my son and daughter a chance to protest. I did once tell my Luca that, had I been an American, he would not have dared make such an important decision without my approval.

When we unpacked our furniture in Milan, I found that we would have to buy more furniture to fill up the new ten-room apartment. I enrolled the children in school and hired a couple and settled down to become a housewife and a hostess for Rizzoli, who wanted Luca and me to do a lot of entertaining.

I had not known Angelo Rizzoli except by reputation as a self-made businessman until one day Luca announced that we were to attend a "command performance" dinner at the Rizzoli home in the center of Milan.

For the occasion I wore a black coat similar to a Jackie Kennedy outfit, typical of the period. When Luca and I arrived at Via del Gesù, the most elegant street in Milan, it was Angelo Rizzoli himself who opened the door, took one look at me, and without another word, turned to my husband and said, "Doesn't your wife own a fur coat?"

I didn't give Luca a chance to answer. "In Rome we don't need fur coats," said I.

Still ignoring me, he told Luca, "Tomorrow I will give you the name of my furrier. Choose the best coat available."

Guess what?

I selected a black mink coat and before long transformed it into the lining of a raincoat. Of course I waited until Luca left the employ of Rizzoli to take this step.

More than fifty years have passed, and although the mink is a bit moth-eaten, it still looks good.

I realized that I was about to begin a new chapter in my life, but before plunging into it I had to return to New York to attend a TWA farewell party in my honor. It took place at the 21 Club, which in the 1960s was still *the* place to go and *the* place to be seen. The Kriendlers, Pete, and Bob, the owners of 21, were good friends. Bob's daughter Karen had spent a year living in Rome when Luca and I both worked for TWA.

Many ex-colleagues and friends attended the event, and of course my Luca was with me, too. It was a fabulous good-bye party. Just some of the guests were William Randolph Hearst, Jr., Oriana Fallaci, Leonard Lyons, Louis Sobol, Earl Blackwell, Bob Considine, and Walter Lippmann. I was totally in my element.

Did I receive a gold watch? No. I had worked for TWA for only nineteen years and nine months—so I didn't qualify!

Back in Milan, my life as a housewife restarted, but it lasted only a few months, until I received a call from the Grand Hotel Villa d'Este. The word was out that I had made a lot of important contacts, so the hotel offered me a PR consulting job, thanks to Jimmy Morton, a TWA passenger and a Villa d'Este guest. I was to bring to Villa d'Este the kind of glamour and panache that had come to TWA during my tenure there.

As far as what Angelo Rizzoli thought about this, he did not protest too much—especially when his wife came to the hotel as a guest, and I took the best possible care of her!

Upon arriving at Villa d'Este in October 1967, I was taken around by the manager of the hotel, Mario Arrigo, to meet all the staff. One of the maids on the first floor was introduced to me as Pina Dombré. She was a sweet lady, elderly and shriveled. I had just met Willy Dombré, who was the general manager for many years, and I couldn't help asking how Pina was connected to him.

Mario explained to me that there was no blood connection. He went on to say that Willy's mother, Clara Dombré, had installed a Swiss housekeeping regime at the Hotel. She personally interviewed and hired the staff. At the time, Pina was barely fourteen years old, so Clara Dombré sort of adopted her and raised her in her home. Pina started working in the hotel only when Clara thought she was ready, and this is how she trained most of the staff. The trial period took place at the Dombré's residence, and Pina became "family." She liked to be known as Pina Dombré. She spent all her life at Villa d'Este and was entirely devoted to the place and to the Dombré family.

Mario and I worked together for many years, and he and I occasionally traveled to foreign countries to promote the hotel. Once, in the United States in the late 1960s, Earl Blackwell, aka "Mr. Celebrity," gave us some assistance. Mario had never been to the U.S. before, so I called all the contacts from my TWA days and was proud to introduce the Villa d'Este manager, who assisted me in promoting Villa d'Este to the "beautiful people" of New York City. Earl suggested that Mario and I give a party at a private club, Raffles, to which Earl belonged (he was a founder, as well). We casually made the invitations by phone—never done in those days—and had a terrific turnout.

And before I go any further, I must introduce my trusted colleague and friend Annamaria Duvia, who also began working at the hotel doing public relations in 1967, just a few weeks before I did. We have been working together all these years, and knows everyone—and everyone knows her. She had planned to retire in 2009, but we refuse to let her go. She is a main contributor to the success of the hotel.

Even though I have now been living on the grounds of the hotel for more than forty years, I still enjoy looking at this heavenly place through the eyes of a photographer or through the description of a writer who has just fallen in love with the "villa on the lake" for the first time. It transports me back to my first visit to the place, which was in the 1950s, when I was working at TWA and had been asked to set up a meeting for the TWA board of directors in Milan. TWA was beginning to run direct flights from New York to Malpensa airport there.

But it was the dead of summer, and too hot to stay in the city, especially when I realized that all the top hotels in the city had no air conditioning. I knew that the board members would not accept a stay in a hotel without air conditioning at that time of year. Then I had a brain wave: I remembered having once visited the grand hotel Villa d'Este. I recalled it as a really magical place situated in a fairy-tale setting and surrounded by a park, described in glowing detail by none other than Edith Wharton, the great traveler and garden lover. Edith Wharton wrote:

> *In the gardens of the Villa d'Este there is much of the Roman spirit—the breadth of design, the unforced inclusion of natural features, and that sensitiveness to the quality of the surrounding landscape which characterizes the great gardens of Campagna.*

Villa d'Este did not have air conditioning in those years, but the location was so sublime and the climate so appealing and Lake Como so glorious that I was complimented for my choice and the meeting was most successful. After that, the directors of the TWA board learned how to fight the heat Italian-style, by keeping the shutters closed during the day and opening them when the sun went down, letting in the cool night breezes.

Once I was settled into my new job at Villa d'Este, my first promotion as PR consultant consisted of sending out a letter to about five hundred contacts I had made during my TWA days. My Luca always said to me, "Everybody loves you because they need you, but the day you leave TWA, your so-called friends will remove your name from their list."

Fearing he might be correct, I sent out a letter saying, "You have probably crossed me off your list of useful contacts, but may I suggest that if you come to Italy you must visit the Grand Hotel Villa d'Este on Lake Como, because I will be there to welcome you and show you around one of the most beautiful spots in the world."

It worked. I don't know whether it was my letter or other factors, but in the years since then Villa d'Este has grown to international acclaim because of the respite it offers from whatever the world of that day might be. Not that Villa d'Este has not been admired for, literally, centuries. Oh, and it has had its moments of notoriety, too. I'll start with a story of admiration, involving Clark Gable. Of course this was before my time at the hotel.

In the early 1950s Clark Gable was in London to collect his customized Jaguar with his companion of the time, Schiaparelli model Suzanne Dadotte. They planned a slow drive to Rome and then on to Naples. By chance Clark Gable and his companion reached Lake Como at a stopping point, and when they saw Villa d'Este they decided to check in for the night. They ended up spending three weeks in heaven, instead of just the stopover originally planned.

Of course, the Villa d'Este golf course, one of the best in the world, provided all the activity and entertainment that Gable was seeking. If it hadn't been for producer Sam Zimbalist, who reminded Gable that he was under contract and to get to Rome *subito* (quickly) to get on the set of *Mogambo* (1953), Gable would have stayed on and on. We still have photos of Clark Gable hanging out in the Villa d'Este clubhouse as a reminder of the "visitor who couldn't leave."

And today we have the new Clark Gable, George Clooney, living just a few villas away, adding continuous sparkle to our glamour. In the last few years, so many stories about Lake Como have appeared in major international magazines that the hotel's reputation continues to grow. In large part this has to do with George Clooney. We even get calls asking to book rooms with a view of Clooney's villa, and sometimes our lake is now referred to as Lake Clooney (as if George Clooney had discovered Lake Como!).

Don't let us forget that if it hadn't been for Cardinal Tolomeo Gallio, Villa d'Este would still be a broken-down convent with lots of little nuns scurrying around. But the publicity, most of it traveling by word of mouth, has helped to build the hotel's reputation, so that in 2009 it was selected The World's Best Hotel by *Forbes Traveler 400*.

Over the years there have been incredible stories of Villa d'Este in the international press. Take the work of Herb Caen, my dear press colleague and friend.

You'll recall I met Herb Caen when I first started working for TWA, so that must have been in the late 1940s. Sometimes known as the Caliph of Bagdad-by-the-Bay, he was an American columnist for the *San Francisco Chronicle* who had the most loyal following in the country and was beloved by all. He was also called the Mr. Big of San Francisco, or simply Mr. San Francisco. His love affair with that city lasted from 1938 until he died in 1997 and was so renowned that the city proclaimed June 14th Herb Caen Day. Seventy-five thousand people turned out on the day the holiday was instituted, to show their affection for the writer.

We were good friends, and when he heard I was doing PR for Villa d'Este, he made a visit to see if he could write about the place and help me out. He came several times, and the following is an excerpt from one of his columns:

> *The first time I went to Villa d'Este at Lake Como I wrote something like, "The exact location of heaven is not known, but it may very well be here," and I see no reason to change that. It remains the benchmark by which all other grand hotels must be measured, only to fall short. Sure, I'm a little prejudiced because my son, Christopher, is a legend there. When, as a little tyke, he first visited the Villa hotel, executive Luca Salvadore asked him, "What do you want to be when you grow up?" "Italian," replied Christopher.*

After my Luca died, Herb wrote me the most touching letter. I thought it important to include an excerpt here because this represents a Herb Caen that not many were fortunate enough to get to know; the sentimental side of Caen. Here's part of it:

Damn! I sit here on a rainy day and think about all the good
times we had, and what a wonderful fellow he was—his
intelligence, his generous spirit, his forever pretending to
be such a "tough guy" when he was a creampuff through
and through.

Herb turned out to be one of Villa d'Este's most avid fans and returned
many a time. Another excerpt from one of his columns:

Villa d'Este: with its roots that go back to the sixteenth
century, its halls echoing with the silent laughter and tears
of pampered princesses, conniving priests, and political
plotters whose portraits frown down from the walls, watching
as a Japanese visitor prowls the hotel and its gardens,
jotting down every detail, for his group wants to replicate
the Villa d'Este in Japan.
"It will never work," Jean Salvadore of the hotel staff
assures him. "You do not have an Italian soul."
He sighs but carries on.

In 1971, I was thinking of how could I promote the hotel in an elegant
way, without resorting to the usual props. I got all my friends interested
in the project, which still had to be worked out, and my friend Harry
Bailey, who had been appointed representative for Christie's auction
house of London, came to my rescue. It turned out that Christie's was
looking for a venue at which to hold its first auction in Europe after the
end of the second world war.

"You've got it made," I told Bailey. "Come to Villa d'Este and I promise
you the auction will be a success." And it was, as predicted.

Collectors and buyers arrived from all parts of the world to attend
the Christie's auction, because the main attraction was a Gian Lorenzo
Bernini model for his famed sculpture, the Fountain of the Four Rivers.
The actual sculpture is found in Rome's Piazza Navona and supports an
ancient Egyptian obelisk over a hollowed-out rock, surmounted by four
marble figures symbolizing four major rivers of the world. This fountain

is one of Bernini's most acclaimed works, and it was first presented to Pope Innocent X in the year 1647. The model to be auctioned was seventy-seven inches high, sculpted in wood and terracotta, gilded, colored, and perfectly preserved. It had remained in the pope's family for nearly three hundred years. The fact that it was at Villa d'Este for an auction created quite a stir and started my years at the hotel off on the right foot. Clients and friends of ours were trying to get an invitation, and the elite all got to know Villa d'Este, if they didn't already know it.

One of my other press colleagues from TWA days, Stan Delaplane, was also a great help in spreading the word of Villa d'Este to a wider audience. Stan visited with me several times. One time he wrote a whole column about the hotel and wrote that if more information was needed, readers should write directly to Jean Govoni Salvadore. I received hundreds of letters. It was amazing how the hotel filled up thanks to Stan and, of course, to Herb Caen. Thanks to them, we soon became known as San Francisco on Lake Como. To this day, a large number of our visitors are from California, probably because of the inspiration they received from American journalists advising them to make what, in the early years, was a very long trip indeed.

But it took a while for the hotel to get the initial buzz going after the war, as it took time for the owners of the hotel, the Dombré family, to get it back into working order. Finally in 1948 the hotel reopened after they had restored the building from top to bottom. Then, on September 16, 1948, during the first major postwar event at Villa d'Este, a fashion show, a murder took place. But more about that later. Now, a little wartime history and how Villa d'Este played into it.

When Mussolini declared war on France and England from the balcony of his study on Piazza Venezia in Rome on June 10, 1940, the hotel lost its international clientele and nearly went out of business. However, by 1942, when Milan was under siege, many of the richest families fled the city and took up residence at Villa d'Este. Notwithstanding the war, this was a time when the hotel was again "swinging." Every night was a party.

By 1943, the Allied forces were pushing back the Germans from the South, so that German control was limited to the North. At this point, the Germans took control of Villa d'Este, the guests were evacuated, and the hotel became a hospital where plastic surgery was performed. It was rumored that before escaping to South America, senior Nazi officials stopped off at Villa d'Este to have their faces remade. It is possible that here many notorious Nazis became unrecognizable.

Finally, in April 1945, the Germans fled the American Fifth Army; the Americans arrived in Cernobbio, and Villa d'Este was liberated along with the rest of the North. According to a July 1945 *New York Times* article, Villa d'Este became the favorite rest camp for GIs on leave.

By 1948, the hotel had been returned to its prewar owners and restored. A big event was scheduled for September of that year because this was the month when the "beautiful people" planned their lake vacations. Biki, the top Milanese couturier of the time, had sent out more than two hundred invitations for a black-tie gala dinner and fashion show to take place on September 15th. Her guest list included luminaries like Baron de Rothschild of Paris, who was known never to miss a good party.

Other interesting guests were the Count Lamberto Bellentani and his wife Pia. The Bellentanis were part of the new "café society" that had cropped up during the war years, and they were seated at a table with silk manufacturer Carlo Sacchi and his wife.

For the previous three years, it had been rumored that Pia and Carlo were in the throes of an affair. This was news, but not shocking; at the time, extramarital affairs were quite common and accepted in high society, as long as they were conducted with certain discretion.

The problem was that Pia had fallen in love with Sacchi. Even knowing that he was unreliable and rather vulgar, she believed that she could "redeem" him.

Dinner went smoothly; the fashion show was a success, but by two o'clock in the morning, the crowds had started thinning out. The Bellentanis and the Sacchis decided to have a drink in the nightclub, and others followed suit. The scenario rapidly unfolded: A shot was fired. Carlo Sacchi was lying on his back on the dance floor, but the orchestra continued to play. At first, it appeared as though Sacchi was playing one of his practical jokes because he appeared to be grinning. Then Pia cried, "It's jammed! It's jammed!" As she held the loaded pistol to her head, everyone now realized that something ghastly had just happened. Biki's husband began to slap Pia repeatedly; three ladies bent over Sacchi's body; the police arrived; Count Bellentani paced the hall, chain smoking.

Both Bellentanis were eventually arrested: Pia for murder, the count for carrying a handgun without a license. It turned out that Carlo Sacchi had been torturing Pia with promises of running away together—promises that he dashed with ridicule during the party that night at Villa d'Este. The final straw came when he called her a *terrona* (a peasant from the South). Insulted and hurt, Pia fired one shot at her lover through her white ermine cape. Naturally, the press had a field day with the events of the evening, trumpeting, A Convent SchoolGirl at Villa d'Este, The Madame Bovary of Villa d'Este, Drama at Villa d'Este, and, most embarrassingly, Countess Kills Lover Who Called Her *Terrona*.

Every year, come September 15th, the press starts calling me to double check the story, which created such a stir more than sixty-two years ago. The protagonists are all dead, but the story is still in great demand.

Through the years Villa d'Este has become renowned for its parties. The most talked-about party during my tenure was probably the Villa d'Este centennial, in 1973. To celebrate the reopening of Villa d'Este and its hundredth-season birthday, a party was organized that would be remembered for many decades to come. The other party that is still talked about was our millennium party, to celebrate the new millennium in the year 2000.

The main event of the first, the hundredth anniversary festivity, was the installation of an indoor pool. All the staff members were instructed how to carry out their duties around the new pool. We already had the only floating pool on Lake Como, but this gave us indoor and outdoor swimming. Nearly two thousand invitations were sent, and it looked as though everyone was accepting. Two orchestras would be playing. On June 26, 1973, at eight p.m., the gates opened to a very elegant crowd.

The flower arrangements were ready and the only worry was the weather. Well, someone up there was watching over us because the weather was perfect. The food and drinks were abundant and excellent and the party went on until early morning when only a few guests remained and we all went to the kitchen to share breakfast.

Visits to the kitchen became a habit during the summer months when our frequent guests returned year after year. We would improvise a midnight spaghetti party. Our favorite dish was Spaghetti Aglio Olio e Peperoncino, which is spaghetti with garlic, olive oil, and chili peppers. The millennium party was equally elaborate and exciting. Ever since Luca had died in 1988, I had spent the holidays in New York City with friends and family. Usually Villa d'Este closes for the season before the end of November and reopens in March, so with nobody around for the holidays, it can become somewhat isolated. At times I rather enjoy living within the famed Villa d'Este mosaic wall, one of the most photographed monuments in the world, but having to spend three to four winter months there, especially if the weather is not at its best, can be quite dreary when you have to turn on lights around three p.m.

But for the turn of the millennium, it was a different story. For the first time in the history of Villa d'Este, the hotel remained open for Christmas and New Year's. We invited only a limited number of guests, all friends. It was like a private party and the results were wonderful: Five unforgettable days in the magical fairy-tale atmosphere of the hotel. One of the attractions was a fashion show created especially for us by Lorenzo Riva, the fashion designer who has become known as the creator of the most beautiful wedding gowns. He spends every weekend at the hotel because he gets his inspiration sitting on the lakefront, watching the world go by. There was also a "night at the opera," with a performance of *La Traviata* and other special evenings enjoyed by one and all. It's a pity that this event can take place only once every thousand years!

These occasions got me to thinking back about when I first arrived on Lake Como and took up residence at Villa d'Este. When I had moved to the premises from Milan after I'd been working at the hotel for about two years, I was anxious to meet some of the local people. I was fortunate enough to be introduced to Carla Porta Musa. We immediately became close friends.

Today Carla is a most attractive, bright, and dynamic 108-year-old lady you will ever meet. She is still writing novels and composing poems. To give you an idea of her vitality, her *joie de vivre:* she underwent a hip replacement when she was already ninety-nine years old. I had just had successful hip replacement surgery, and when Carla heard that I was as good as new, she decided she too could have a successful replacement, notwithstanding doctors, family, and friends trying to dissuade her from having this operation.

"Giovanna had her hip replacement, and look at her, she is fine," said Carla. We tried to explain to Carla that she could be my mother, based on her chronological age! Carla would not listen to reason. She was adamant. She called the surgeon who had operated on me, and although he tried to talk Carla out of this folly, she insisted!

"Worst comes to worst, I'll die on the operating table, and I couldn't think of a better way to go. I've been so lucky and I've had a wonderful and most rewarding life," she said as she announced her final decision.

She sailed through with flying colors!

Her one hundreth birthday took place on March 15, 2002 with a lunch at Villa d'Este. Nearly thirty people attended, including the Mayor of Como. It was a lovely day, and sun poured into the Veranda restaurant. When the birthday cake was wheeled in by Luciano Parolari, our popular executive chef, everybody rose to cheer and all the restaurant staff gathered around to sing "Happy Birthday." As I looked around I caught a glimpse of Chelsea Clinton, daughter of former President Bill Clinton and Secretary of State Hillary Clinton, seated with a friend at a table close to ours.

I asked the maitre d' to invite Chelsea to come over for a taste of the cake. Chelsea, who was a guest of Donatella Versace, sister of Gianni, the designer whose villa was around the bend on Lake Como, decidedly enjoyed the cake. She came over to our table and got down on her knees to thank Carla and wish her a happy birthday.

Everybody was most taken by Chelsea and the general comment was that she was well brought up and knew how to behave, which is not surprising considering the charm quotient of both parents.

In all of my chatter about the hotel itself, I may have forgotten to mention the guests, Chelsea Clinton being but the tip of the iceberg. Villa d'Este guests come for all sorts of reasons and sometimes they provide the interest and entertainment; and sometimes it's the hotel that does that job. Sometimes they're famous and sometimes not. But

I do think that they universally enjoy their visits. Some of them have been coming for thirty years or more, and some are just one-time visitors. They come for relaxation, romance, vacation, work-related stays on editorial, publicity, or promotional junkets, conventions, and the food—sometimes to have it cooked by us and sometimes to take lessons from our kitchen. But whatever their mission, the hotel has done its utmost to make sure that everyone has a memorable time and I, of course, have had the opportunity to rub shoulders with some of the most interesting people in the world.

I think I'll start with the English couple who came for romance.

Lake Como is known as the most romantic spot in the world. There are many romantic stories that remind us of Somerset Maugham's books. One story is about an English lady who came year after year with her husband, a lord and a producer. She met and fell madly in love with Gildo, an ex-boxer whose job at the hotel was to invite the lady guests to dance and keep them entertained.

The lady (whose name I will omit) and Gildo ran off, leaving husband and son to take care of themselves. Not long after, the lord died, leaving the lady penniless—and so the two lovers roamed from one place to another, getting odd jobs as entertainers. Then they decided to return to Cernobbio to open a pub opposite the Villa d'Este gates. It was attractively decorated, but the lovers had no idea how to run the place. It didn't succeed, and it was rumored that they both took to drink. They soon went bankrupt, and it seems that Gildo committed suicide, although no one knows what happened to the lady. It was a Villa d'Este beginning with a sad ending.

Every year we have a number of annual events that occur at the hotel. One of these is our famous Fourth of July celebration. A wonderful dinner is served, usually outside on the grounds; music is played; and the party ends with a gorgeous fireworks display over Lake Como. One of my favorite "party" stories of Villa d'Este relates to the guests, as they usually do.

As far back as I can remember, Peggy and Louis Sobol were permanent fixtures at Villa d'Este during the month of July. Sobol, whose column appeared in the *New York Journal American,* was a creature of habit. He and his spouse arrived punctually, just in time for the July 4th party, every year. This is one of our major fetes and the Sobols always took the same room, the same table at the bar, the same table at the Terrace restaurant, and the same table in the Veranda restaurant. But there was one year when a strike was called in all the hotels throughout Italy. Our staff tried to get out of it, but the unions were on the watch. Every hotel had to comply, including Villa d'Este. Only the staff who had managerial jobs were allowed to work, and they arrived for their jobs in civilian clothes. We informed our clientele about the situation, and they were all very understanding. Some even offered to help out.

I took some clients who were friends to the kitchen. Our chef, Luciano, joined us and had us all preparing dishes of cold cuts, prosciutto, salami, sausages, salads, vegetables, fruit, and plenty of home-made ice cream and cookies. We set up everything buffet style, then sat down to eat together.

It was like a private party; we all got to know one another, and we made more friends in one day than if our guests had been with us for a month. The wives of the employees came and made up the beds. It was fun to see VIPs like the Sobols carrying around platters of food and serving other guests. We all had a great time.

When the Sobols left, they asked us to let them know if there was to be another strike, because they would fly over to participate. "It was great fun—the best time we've ever had!"

Ian Forbes, CEO and parent board member of large international trading groups, and his charming wife, Judith, came for an annual visit to Villa d'Este for more than thirty years. Ian was originally from Scotland, but the couple lived in Australia. They would spend the summer on the lake and hardly ever left the premises. They even ate most of their meals at the hotel, they enjoyed it so much.

They always arrived in June together with a whole group of friends they had made while sunning at the pool in earlier visits. It became a sort of tradition for all the returning guests to have their meals at the same time. Cocktails together, separate tables for dinner, then dancing under the stars on the terrace overlooking the lake. It was quite a wonderful reunion for all of them, and for those of us permanently on the hotel's premises as well.

Oriana Fallaci and William Randolph Hearst, Jr. at the author's farewell party from TWA at 21 Club in New York City, 1966.

Left: The author and her husband at the farewell party, she wearing the plaid dress she designed for the earlier visit of the Queen of England to Rome in 1961.

Above: Ellen Tannen with her family member, Bob Kriendler, proprietor of 21 Club.

The "very beautiful" Rosemary Wilson with her husband, Earl, along with Leonard Lyons *(right)*, no doubt exchanging Hollywood gossip at the 21 Club party.

Luca Salvadore and Leo Rosten at the 21 Club party.

Right: The location of the author's house was originally a greenhouse at Villa d'Este.

Above: Luca on the water at Villa d'Este.

Herb Caen was a frequent visitor to Villa d'Este since the author's arrival there in 1967; Caen had been a good friend from her TWA days.

The 1971 Christie's auction held at Villa d'Este was one of the first "launch" events held by the author to bolster the visibility of the world class hotel to a wider audience.

Left: Alfred Hitchcock was a frequent and welcome visitor to Villa d'Este.

Above: Clark Gable and the hotel concierge became well acquainted after Gable had stayed at the hotel for a few weeks.

The famed pool on the lake is as beautiful from above as it is at eye-level and remains the only floating pool on the lake to this day.

Cernobbio - Lago di Como Villa d'Este - Il mosaico

A postcard image of the mosiac, built in 1568, one of the most
photographed monuments in Italy.

TRY A PALACE FOR SIZE

SIGNORA JEAN SALVADORE wears a lifetime on her wrist.

It takes the form of six bracelets of charms and mementos from her personal life, her tours around the world and her 22 years in public relations.

She is in Melbourne this week under the sponsorship of Allitalia, the Italian airline, to promote the luxury holiday area of the Lake Como area, and in particular, Villa d'Este, on Lake Como.

She arrived in Melbourne complete with a short film of Villa d'Este, which is a frankly luxury hotel, catering for people (and their pets) in the grand manner.

On film, the Villa d'Este looks like the last world in gracious living. An old and beautiful palace, once owned by a Queen of England, with plenty of outdoor activities in clean, pure air, and 20 minutes away from the great casinos of Switzerland.

It caters for tastes ranging from formal dining, through casual eating to discotheques, ("away from the main building, so as not to disturb the clientele"), says Signora Salvadore.

It is an eye opener to realise that basic tariff for Villa d'Este is U S $40 a day, which is rather less than the top prices demanded by some Australian hotels.

The only snag is you have to get to Italy first.

The author's first travels to Australia in 1970 were newsworthy in Melbourne's newspaper, *The Sun,* when the author traveled there to promote Villa d'Este.

Australians of note are frequent visitors to the hotel from the early days of the author's arrival. *Above:* with Mary Rossi, the noted Australian travel agent and *left:* and Elizabeth Rich and Sir Ronald Alfred "Ron" Brierley.

Above and right: The results of Helmut Newton's famous "sneak attack" photos taken at Villa d'Este and unknown to the author until she attended his book signing in New York City, in which they appeared.

The Versace family and Kirk Douglas and his wife choose the same spot to have their photo taken at Villa d'Este, on the shore of Lake Como.

Longtime friends Larry Ashmead and Walter Matthews only visited Villa d'Este once in the early 1990s, but they became so enchanted by Italy that they purchased a villa of their own in Tuscany.

David Brown and wife Helen Gurley Brown, the renowned editor of Cosmopolitan magazine, visited Villa d'Este and made a side visit to Comacina Island, the only island in Lake Como, and ate at the Locanda dell'Isola Comacina restaurant, where this photograph was taken.

Above: Robert Mitchum and *right:* Bette Davis: Both were visitors to
Villa d'Este and each created something of a sensation because of their
distinctive personalities.

Carla Porta Musa is a legend in Como and is at the writing of this book 107 years old. Here, she celebrates three birthdays at Villa d'Este with Villa d'Este President/CEO Jean-Marc Droulers.

Chelsea Clinton, who happened to be visiting on Porta Muso's 100th birthday, joined the party to extend birthday wishes.

The author with Carla Porta Musa.

Even in 1939 Villa d'Este served as the perfect backdrop for high fashion photography shoots.

Right: In 1993 the Droulers twins, Virginie and Nathalie, modeled fashions of the great Italian designer Roberto Capucci at Villa d'Este.

Fashionable guests at Villa d'Este surround Bernard Leser, the founder of *Vogue* Australia. They include, from left, Nathalie Droulers, the author, Leser, Marta Hallett, Virginie Droulers, and Mary Ellen Barton.

Local legendary fashion designer Lorenza Riva is seen here with vocalist Edda Pusceddu, the author, and Luigi Valietti. The ladies are wearing dresses designed by Riva.

The author with Judith Forbes, who, with her husband, Ian hosted the author's 70th birthday party at Villa d'Este.

Sylvester Stallone takes advantage of the vast hotel grounds for excericse.
Here he is at the foot of the Hercules statue.

Lady Bird Johnson came to Villa d'Este after reading the author's previous book, Villa d'Este Style.

Newlywed Kristi Yamaguchi arrived at Villa d'Este in 2001 with her husband and fellow Olympic medal winter, Bret Hedican; here with the author.

Villa d'Este is known for its extraordinary grounds as much as for its food, location, and service. Here more than 500-year-old plane tree commands a majestic view of the entire property.

The first to arrive was the famed heart transplant surgeon, Dr. Christiaan Barnard, from South Africa. Other couples came from Florida, New York, and London, and they all stayed for a month or so. But as years went by, the group started thinning out. Christiaan Barnard and Paul Leopold (representative of the Maison Lanvin when Como was the silk center of the world) passed away, and so did Ian Forbes, and their widows did not feel like returning without their better halves. They preferred to keep all those happy memories intact.

Instead a whole different crowd took over, and Villa d'Este was swinging again with a totally different look. It was fashionable to celebrate all occasions, and the season of 1996 was full of happy events. Birthdays were always celebrated and even my seventieth became an event. My son, Andrea, and my daughter, Claudia, were invited; and none other than Jean-Marc Droulers himself, president and chief executive officer of Villa d'Este, made all of the arrangements with the Forbes who hosted the party. A photo of Judith Forbes and me was taken before the dinner, which was served in the Napoleon Room, created for the emperor in 1805.

Luciano went out of his way to make that birthday a festive and elegant occasion. The hotel guests who attended were nearly fifty in number. Everybody had a great time. One guest, as it turned out, was also celebrating her birthday (day and month like mine, only younger). Her name: Anita Draycott, from Toronto.

Ten years later, a fabulous party was arranged for my eightieth birthday. This time it was held in the Empire Room, and there were about thirty-five guests. The theme of the evening was red, my favorite color, and every photograph shows red roses adorning the table. And, of course, I wore red!

Guests came from far and wide: Bruce Jarrett from Australia, Dr. Jim Bonorris and his wife, Lucy Zahran, from California, Edward Deluca from New York, Mary Ellen Barton from London, Maureen Bonini from Ireland. The rest came from Milan, Como, and Varese. It was quite a crowd. What happy memories.

Now people travel vast distances at the drop of a hat, but when I first started traveling for the airlines in the 1950s, it was quite rare to travel at all, never mind traveling long distances. And I did a lot of traveling when working for the airlines.

I visited so many sites that I don't even remember them all. But when I looked through my diaries, I recalled my visit to India in 1971 with a small group of Italian journalists. We were scheduled to interview Prime Minister Indira Gandhi. I thought that I should investigate among the travel agencies whether we could drum up some business for Villa d'Este. I even contacted the Maharajah of Gwalior—a VIP passenger from my TWA days—but I couldn't get him to come and visit Lake Como, because we had no elephants. "No elephants, no visit," was the message conveyed!

Anyway I had a good time despite the fact that we never got to meet Indira Gandhi. Although we didn't get to see her in person, we were well taken care of by her press office. A car was put at our disposal twenty-four hours a day, and every day a program was worked out for us. It was quite an experience and it made us feel like pioneers, as not many Italians were traveling to India in those days.

Nonetheless, the Villa d'Este built up a steady flow of Indian visitors, little by little. The hotel, so very long a place of refuge and tranquillity, has always prided itself on catering to a mixed crowd. Our guests come from all parts of the world, making Villa d'Este quite the vacation melting pot.

Speaking of political luminaries, some years ago I got a phone call out of the clear blue sky from Mrs. Lyndon Johnson. It was Lady Bird Johnson, the widow of the former president, whom I've always admired. At the time she must have been in her late eighties. Mrs. Johnson wanted to know if we had space in the hotel for a visit from her. Of course, I said, but she explained, "I also have bodyguards who don't have to sleep in the hotel." Then she said, "Please talk to my daughter."

Lynda Bird Johnson Robb took over. She explained that her mother had seen my book *Villa d'Este Style* at the home of some friends and she was so taken by the beautiful photos that she declared that she had to visit Villa d'Este while she was still able to get around. She and her daughter spent a whole week discovering the treasures of Lake Como. We lunched and dined together in some of the little local trattorias, along with eating at the hotel.

At the time, Lady Bird Johnson's eyesight was failing rapidly, but she had bodyguards and the Italian police watching out for her.

When necessary, a wheelchair was made available. We enjoyed ourselves, hiding from her bodyguards behind the plants on the Villa d'Este terrace overlooking the lake; naturally they were somewhat concerned when they couldn't see her. It was something of an adult hide-and-seek.

During the 1960s and early 1970s, Alfred Hitchcock and his wife, Alma, would spend a fortnight at Villa d'Este in the month of September. It was their annual holiday, and they always looked forward to it. They never left the premises, and we had to make sure that there would be no paparazzi in sight—otherwise the Hitchcocks would pack up and leave.

Only once did some photographers show up, at the cocktail hour. Hitchcock was about to throw a tantrum, but he calmed down when I told him that the photographers had been hired to cover an important wedding taking place at Villa d'Este. Even if he was recognized, they would ignore him. To this day I wonder whether the great movie director wasn't a bit disappointed that the photographers were not there to see him.

Hitchcock was quite a gourmet, and he had a passion for risotto, which in his day was essentially unknown except in northern Italy. I would accompany Hitchcock to the kitchen every day to confer with the chefs so that Hitchcock could choose his meal. He tasted every kind of risotto, and it became a challenge for our chefs to keep creating new versions, from risotto with white truffles to Milanese risotto with ossobuco.

At the end of one of his stays Hitchcock gave us permission to organize a press conference in the kitchen. What a turnout! Italian television shot a movie, with Hitchcock as the main actor. He donned the chef's toque and chased all the kitchen staff around with a big carving knife.

The cuisine of Villa d'Este and chef Luciano Parolari have become world famous, and their reputation travels with me wherever I go. My last encounter with Walter Cronkite, in fact, was at Artusi, the Villa d'Este-owned restaurant in New York City.

When Walter Cronkite died I realized what a loss it was to all of us. I loved what a reader wrote to the *New York Times:* "I will believe that

Cronkite is gone only if he announces it." I was unaware that he was also well known in Italy, which was evidenced by the many obituaries he received in the Italian papers on his death.

I met him for the first time in 1950 when I was working at TWA. Cronkite was a passenger on the first TWA press flight to Rome, along with Stan Delaplane, Herb Caen, and other top reporters and columnists. Many years went by without being in any contact with him, and then one day in the 1990s I bumped into him in Artusi, located just opposite the CBS building on West 52nd Street. I was so excited to see him again in person that I blurted out, "Mr. Cronkite, do you remember me from 1950 in Rome?"

It was pretentious to expect him to remember me, but he immediately responded, "Of course I remember you."

Naturally I liked him all the more for this gentlemanly response!

Our favorite celebrity visitor, though, bar none, isn't from the Hollywood crowd. He is a musician: Bruce Springsteen. Whenever Bruce Springsteen is on tour in Italy, he travels with his family and he always spends a few days at Villa d'Este.

An episode worthy of mentioning was in 2003: The Boss sang "Backstreets" for a four-year-old fan who was staying at the hotel with her parents.

Visitors usually make a stopover, as well, at Comacina Island in the center of Lake Como, where the famous inn with the only restaurant, Locanda, is to be found. Apart from the fact that the island is breathtaking and very romantic, a visit is a must, and I am happy to recommend it.

I have spent many birthday parties on the island, eating the set menu that has been served since the late 1940s. The food consists of vegetables of the season, ham, and bresaola, followed by lake-native fish, grilled chicken, salad, Parmesan cheese, ice cream, fruit, ceremonial coffee, and plenty of wine. On each visit, The Boss and his family have their photo taken with Benvenuto Puricelli, the current owner, and it is published in the local paper.

The year 2009 was a most successful year from a public relations point of view. Tina Brown, the editor and writer, wrote a great story about Lake Como and Villa d'Este—actually, better still, it was really about Villa d'Este and Lake Como. Tina and her husband, Sir Harold Evans, and family spent a lot of time exploring all little villages and trattorias. She behaved like a tourist and never asked for any VIP treatment.

Anna Wintour was in the hotel at the same time as Tina but didn't stay as long. She seemed to inspect the premises, then left shortly thereafter.

One interesting group of visitors, some years ago now, was Woody Allen and Mia Farrow, with their family of many children. I asked the staff to please ignore them. Of course what I meant was no autographs, no photograph requests—give them the best service but pretend you don't recognize them. It worked out fine.

Woody and Mia's children behaved well. When it was time for lunch and or dinner, the children came marching in wearing their desert boots (it was the height of summer and very hot, too). Once they sat down at the table that had been reserved for them at the far end of the restaurant, they never opened their mouths, except to eat, of course. They seemed to be enjoying their visit.

The day they were leaving, I saw Woody Allen at the concierge desk, which happens to be pretty tall, and I realized how short he was, because his chin just reached the top of the desk. All of a sudden, who comes in by the revolving door but the one and only Arnold Schwarzenegger, a vision of virility—and height! He was wearing Bermudas and an ever-so-tight T-shirt that barely covered his bulging muscles. He looked like Mr. Universe, and without glancing right or left, he marched right past Woody Allen without saying a word. Woody Allen was aware of Schwarzenegger's presence and looked up at him. Woody seemed to have shrunk.

It was quite a scene with Maria Shriver trailing behind Arnold throughout the Schwarzeneggers' stay. Arnold wore a T-shirt most of the time. His children were well behaved, and they also had a great time and seemed to get along with the hotel guests.

In looking through my thousands of photos of my life, I could not find a photo of Robert De Niro, although he has visited Villa d'Este in both 2008 and 2009. Like Hitchcock, he made a point of warning us that if we let any of the paparazzi in, he and his family would pack up and leave.

Of course we would never do that. We have always been able to maintain the privacy of all our guests since the hotel first opened, in 1873. In an effort to comply with his wishes, whenever he wanted to enjoy his meals on the terrace overlooking the lake, we always surrounded the movie star and his family with plants and a tent so he could eat in peace, without anybody seeing him.

One day he wanted to visit a trattoria located opposite Villa d'Este on Lake Como, and he requested that there should not be anybody else in the restaurant when he and his family were there. Because he was told that this was impossible, he decided to have the place opened up early so he and his family could at least taste the appetizers, and they would leave when the customers began to arrive. Apparently this precaution was not necessary, as when the restaurant did open, De Niro and his family ate in peace with total anonymity.

Barbra Streisand is another guest who becomes highly agitated when she sees a photographer or someone seeking her autograph.

I first met Barbra Streisand and her husband, James Brolin, when I greeted them upon their arrival at the hotel in 1999. Well-known travel agent Bill Fischer asked me to take care of her because she only had my name as a contact. Whenever she was in touch, she would telephone and address me as Mrs. Salvadore. Nobody has ever referred to me as Mrs. Salvadore! I couldn't help remarking how well she had been brought up. I was more than honored, and I really enjoyed being with her and her husband.

Unlike the two celebrities mentioned earlier, the great musician Billy Joel is a frequent visitor to the hotel who exhibits no fears or anxieties, no airs, and he is a pleasure to have "in the house," as they say. I was reminded recently by Danilo Zucchetti, our manager, of how generous Billy Joel is when he comes to the hotel. He arrives from the airport by helicopter, and he is always very unassuming. He's a very quiet and elegant fellow, and never makes extraordinary demands.

But besides just being a "regular guest," he provides entertainment on occasion, which is exciting to all involved. We have a wonderful piano bar most evenings, either at our inside bar or on the terrace overlooking the lake, with local entertainment that is quite good. On occasion, Billy Joel takes over the piano and entertains the guests.

As I reflect back, I realize how lucky I am to have met this wagonload of celebrities during my time both at TWA and Villa d'Este. They have all had an influence on my life.

But it's not all Hollywood at Villa d'Este. In fact, one of the reasons we have been able to draw so many interesting and influential people over the years is that for centuries the best quality silk has been produced on Lake Como. This means that for many decades during my tenure here, some of the most regular guests have been textile and fashion people from around the world. Many came for the shows that used to take place twice every year.

In 1993, Villa d'Este hosted an exhibition of fifty gala evening gowns of the great fashion creator Roberto Capucci, whose sculpturelike clothes are an absolute triumph in the use of silk fabrics. He is not only a designer but a technical genius, although he doesn't sew his own fashions. Each of his pleated gowns and cloaks, all hand-sewn, requires approximately two hundred yards of silk and three months of hand labor. Capucci, who is considered one of the all-time greatest fashion designers, readily admits that it has become more and more difficult to find the skilled workers needed to sew his fashions.

Today there has been a slowdown in textile "traffic." China has become very competitive and the world financial crisis has hit all textile manufacturers, many of whom who are having a hard time surviving.

But at its apex in the 1970s, the silk industry flourished. Twice a year, an important event known as IdeaComo was held at Villa d'Este, and Como became the textile center of the world. During these events the hotel was closed to the public, the rooms were emptied out, and the many silk manufacturers moved in. Visitors, only upon invitation, came from all parts of the world and looked forward to doing business at Villa d'Este. Many returned as clients to enjoy Villa d'Este on a vacation. Bill Blass was one of them. Others were Oleg Cassini, Karl Lagerfeld, Yves Saint Laurent, Pierre Cardin, Gianfranco Ferré, and Gianni Versace.

Antonio Ratti, the number one textile manufacturer, ran the show, and not only did he have a passion for silk as art, he also cultivated the arts in general. He founded the Antonio Ratti Textile Center at the Metropolitan Museum of Art in New York City, charged with the mission of studying and preserving fabrics.

When Ratti died, his daughter, Annie, took over. IdeaComo moved from its Villa d'Este location to Villa Erba, as a matter of convenience to hotel guests. Villa Erba is Luchino Visconti's former home, and it is practically next door to the hotel, but somehow the new plans didn't work out. I guess that after experiencing the elegant style of Villa d'Este, which was and still is the major attraction of the hotel, Villa Erba seemed to pale by comparison. Beppe Modenese, known as the Prime Minister of Italian Fashion, and Franco Savorelli di Bertinoro were in charge of IdeaComo public relations, and they did a fabulous job.

Fashion shows were originally born in Florence and stayed there, thanks to Emilio Pucci, until they became so abundant that it was necessary to move them all to Milan. Some fashion houses, such as Valentino and Sorelle Fontana, Ava Gardner's favorite designer, remained in Rome.

At the end of the 2007 season, we introduced the Chef's Table promotion, based on a style of dining that we had learned about when we were invited to prepare a few gala dinners for the fiftieth anniversary of the United Nations. That is how Luciano Parolari and I met Julia Child, the great American cooking doyenne.

Our first Chef's Table at Villa d'Este was initiated as an occasion to do something special for our 108-year-old friend Carla Porta Musa, who at the time was a mere 105 years young.

We explained to Carla, who may be aged but is still sharp as a tack, that eating in the kitchen with the chef was all the rage in New York. Since we Italians like to keep up with "the Joneses," meaning "the Americans," she gladly accepted.

She was seated at the kitchen table with Jean-Marc Droulers to her right. Raffaella Bruni, the wife of the mayor of Como, Stefano Bruni, attended as well, and we had a jolly good time. Naturally, other hotels copied us, but as always, we were the first!

One of the great treasures of Villa d'Este, other than the natural ones of environment and weather, is the cuisine that is available not only at the hotel itself, but in the region. Italy is known for its great food, but the north has a special place in the heart of food lovers because the cuisine is distinctively similar to Austro-Hungarian cooking in its use of potatoes, pork, and cabbage. North-central Italy (the Villa d'Este region) is famous for risotto and other rice dishes, as well as veal, wonderful cheeses, and dairy products due to large-scale cattle ranching. Central Italian cuisine is noted for pasta and wild boar, while the coastal areas are known for its fish and seafood.

In 1966, when I had to say good-bye to my beloved Rome and get ready to take up residence in Milan, I had mixed feelings about this transfer. But I took the attitude that, at the age of forty, it was time to start a new life. The speed with which the transition happened was a blessing, because I didn't get a chance to think it over too much. Besides, there was no decision to make. And before we actually moved to Milan, Luca and I had the good fortune to spend a weekend at Villa d'Este, just to try to get some sense of the lifestyle in Milan.

We went, we fell in love with Villa d'Este, and when I was offered the job as public relations consultant, I accepted. As I mentioned, a friend and passenger on TWA, Jimmy Morton, had given my name to the management as a candidate for this work. I was already somewhat familiar with Villa d'Este, having visited there in the 1950s when attending business trips to Milan. Who wouldn't like to stay and work at the hotel on Lake Como?

Once I accepted the consultancy and took off my housewife's apron, I was thrilled with my new venture, and I plunged with gusto into promoting the hotel. How presumptuous of me, and more important, how ironic, as I didn't even know how to boil water!

Let me open a parenthesis: In the 1970s, we added cuisine "All-Americana" at the pool bar, serving hot dogs, hamburgers, club sandwiches, banana splits, and so on. When our executive chef, who was half French (and thus very proper in his approach to cuisine!), saw that these dishes, new to Villa d'Este, were successful, he wrote out a new menu that offered a home-made banana split. At the same time, we decided to introduce genuine Italian food, which was completely ignored until we ran a terrific campaign. Everyone loves Italian food, and the food of the north is distinctively different from the more commonly known southern cuisines at that time.

Villa d'Este had a first-rate kitchen serving classic dishes of the region. Why not start a cooking school for visitors to the hotel as well? What we did was brilliant: We had cooking classes for the locals who wanted to find out how to cook "All-Americana."

In all the years that I worked for TWA from 1946 to 1966, I had it made. Most of the time publicists of those days would come to me with their ideas, and I just had to choose what I deemed best.

However, at this stage in life I had to find or make up something new. It came to me all of a sudden: a cooking school! When I announced it at the Villa d'Este board meeting, the board members who were all pretty close to eighty, looked at me, rather startled, and said, "Great! But who is going to run it?"

My answer was: "I will, of course!"

And this is how it developed. I had never been interested in cooking, and least of all in eating. I was married to a gourmet who was a fanatic about his food. That is why we always employed a cook (fifty years ago it was not considered an extravagance) who loved to spoil my Luca.

I looked around the hotel kitchens to choose a cook for my classes, since I was completely unable to give a demonstration on my own. With the help of the general manager, Mario Arrigo, we started giving classes to the local people who belonged to the sporting club.

I would do the talking and the chef would do the cooking. Many members were attracted because we taught dishes typical of foreign countries such as India, China, Spain, and mostly France. We had a great time and word got around, so we soon received invitations from the States to prepare benefit dinners. Before we knew it, Julie Dannenbaum invited us to appear at her Philadelphia Cooking School.

Our travels to America expanded. I had met Mitch Miller on several occasions in the 1950s and in the 1960s when he was one of the most influential figures in American popular music. He was considered the best classical oboist in the United States. He was very popular and had a long period of glory when *Sing Along with Mitch* ran on television in the early 1960s. The last time I saw him was in 1977 when Luciano Parolari was invited to Cincinnati as a special guest for a Bella Notte bash. It was a happening at Shillito's department store in the Kenwood mall.

The store closed, and this is when Luciano and I prepared as many desserts as we could . . . until we discovered that instead of using sugar we had used salt. The bins all looked alike! Luckily we still had all night to prepare a new set of shortcake tarts.

The reason that I bring up this episode is because Luciano did not bat an eye at this turn of events. He calmed me down, and we went back to baking. Of course Villa d'Este's contribution was greatly appreciated and we managed to laugh off our embarrassment, which we kept secret until today.

For many years we spent the winter, when the hotel was closed, traveling around the world to give cooking lessons. Luciano was a big hit everywhere we went, and after forty-three years at Villa d'Este, he is still going strong. Naturally he paved the way for other entrepreneurs, hotels, restaurants, and individuals to introduce a large choice of Italian dishes in new places.

Everyone knows Marcella Hazan, of course, and another Italian who loves to teach cooking is Giuliano Bugialli, the Renaissance expert from Florence. His books, written in English, are well known in the food world, although not so much in Italy. However, his fame has finally reached the Italians, who are beginning to take an interest in cooking—previously considered strictly a woman's chore—and more cooking schools are popping up all over the country.

I like to credit Villa d'Este as a leader in this phenomenon, paving the way for both gourmets and beginners, who realized that they had a passion they could develop. Food has become so important in all cultures now, with so much skill everywhere that there is almost no need to travel to Bologna to taste an authentic Lasagne alla Parmigiana or to Milan for a true risotto. It seems that eventually there will be no distinction between northern and southern cooking in Italy. Local foods always give an extra thrill to a dish, though, and this is why Luciano has created his own kitchen garden on the grounds of the hotel, so he always has fresh herbs.

Our first cooking school started with a Christmas menu featuring Italian specialties. The classes were a big success almost overnight and by 1973, when Villa d'Este celebrated its one hundredth anniversary as a hotel, cooking classes were in full swing. Not only were the kitchens of Villa d'Este crowded with Americans and Australians, but the invitations for Luciano to give demonstrations to various benefits around the world kept pouring in.

The food craze was just beginning in America in 1973. At that time, only James Beard, Craig Claiborne, and Julia Child had national reputations. But then the scene exploded, and chefs like Dannenbaum, Jacques Pepin, and others would change everyone's opinion about home cooking. Many Americans got their inspiration from the cooking classes at Villa d'Este, where Luciano Parolari was teaching inspired northern Italian cooking and running exchange cooking classes with noted chefs and kitchens in America as well.

In November 1976, when the hotel closed for the season, I started planning (with the aid of Chef Luciano Parolari) a cooking tour which developed into a fantastic promotion. It began when Stan Swinton, the Associated Press general manager in Italy, called me to book a suite at Villa d'Este for William S. Morris III, one of the members of the Associated Press Board, and his wife Sissie. I promised to look after the Morrises and I was with them most of the time. We tried all the restaurants and trattorias in the area together.

As we had been going out for dinner every night, I decided to invite them to my house for a home-cooked meal. They happily accepted and after we had eaten, Sissie asked me, "Do you always cook like this?" She then popped another question and asked if I would be willing to give a cooking demonstration to raise funds for the Augusta (Georgia) Symphony Orchestra of which she was the President.

I responded, "I would be delighted to organize it all but I would like Chef Luciano to accompany me and while he is doing the cooking, I will do the commentary."

We arrived in Augusta and we were greeted so warmly that we couldn't wait to visit the city and get to know the rest of the Morris family. Before the demonstration took place, we were hosted with a dinner party that included a couple of hundred guests. I don't remember the exact number, but it looked like anybody and everybody who was interested in Villa d'Este's cuisine was there and believe me, it was quite a crowd.

Of course, Luciano's performance was greatly applauded and Billy talked us into staying overnight in his home. What a nice surprise! Billy wanted to take us to his plantation and give us a taste of Southern hospitality. It was an experience I'll truly never forget.

Suddenly Italian food became very trendy and Italian restaurants were popping up all over. Today, spaghetti and meatballs do not appear on the menu any longer. That was a dish for the migrants of a hundred years ago. We have all become so sophisticated. Nearly fifty years have gone by, and Luciano Parolari is still with Villa d'Este. He has collaborated on cookbooks that are making their way around the world: *Cooking Ideas from Villa d'Este,* my original compilation of recipes in the 1970s from his recipes; later, *The Villa d'Este Cookbook;* and most recently, *Tales of Risotto,* focusing on the specialty of the region, with recipes by a chef who has been dubbed the "King of Risotto."

How did this love for food become such an obsession? I think that the war years, when we learned what the word "hunger" meant, the rumbling stomach—that is a sensation that stays with one for a lifetime. When my mother met Luca, she said to me, "Remember, the way to a man's heart is through his stomach!" She was right.

One of my first VIPs when I started my career at TWA was Helen McCully from Amherst, Nova Scotia, who lived all her life in New York. She was known as one of the best food writers in America and held the influential position as food editor at *House Beautiful* magazine.

When I had been at TWA, Helen had been sent to Rome by the magazine on an article assignment with photographer Fons Iannelli, to do an article based on the theme "family style" cooking, and as the example of people who lived this cooking were a friends of mine, antiques dealer Marcello and Lina Terenzi. Luca and I were the guests for the faux dinner party arranged for the photo shoot. I remember Melanzane alla Parmigiana (eggplant parmesan) was served, a specialty of the Emilia region of Italy, the food of which was virtually unknown in the States and even in many parts of Italy in the 1950s.

But this was the moment that the Salvadore and McCully friendship was born. It lasted until 1977 when Helen, age seventy-five, passed away. I miss her, and I shall never forget how she helped us to promote the Villa d'Este kitchen and its cuisine in America. She made sure we were invited, repeatedly, to the States. I dedicated *Cooking Ideas from Villa d'Este* to Helen and to my husband Luca.

It was Helen who sent James Beard to Villa d'Este, asking me to watch over him and make sure he didn't eat or drink too much. I did my best, but Jim caught on and said that he would eat and drink as much as he wanted. He wasn't a small man and he said he needed hearty meals to sustain himself. At that point in his life, it was unlikely that I would be able to moderate his intake!

But Beard really went out of his way to be supportive, and he wrote a wonderful article about risotto, which was unknown to Americans at the time, for *Gourmet* magazine. The article included a recipe for risotto with smoked salmon, and the dish was photographed for the cover of the December 1972 issue. After that, this dish appeared on our daily menu, and it became known as Risotto à la James Beard.

In 1995, when the United Nations celebrated its fiftieth anniversary, Luciano Parolari was invited to New York for a whole month to prepare gala dinners at the United Nations. The invitation came directly from Sylvia Fuhrman, assistant to Kofi Annan, who has since become a good friend. Sylvia is in her nineties and still works at the U.N. Around the same time, the Chef's Table at the United Nations became very popular; Julia Child was the guest of honor on one occasion. I was very thrilled to meet her, and she was most gracious and pleasant. Julia's reputation grew over the years, and she became a true culinary superstar and an icon that many people will never forget.

Like Julia Child, Luciano Parolari, who has been with Villa d'Este for more than forty years, has gained accolades from everyone he has met. His love for food and his humble personality make him one of the great chefs of the world. He's still creating innovative recipes, while giving people the best renditions of the classics of the north at the same time.

As the years go by, thanks to Julia Child (and now Paula Deen), "Butter is back and plenty of it!"

There is a continuing theme of food in my relationship with my best friend, Australian Mary Rossi, who provided me with one of my best stories at our very first dinner together.

I met Mary in the late 1950s, when I still worked for TWA. One day I got a call from the receptionist. A certain Mary Rossi, referred to me by Maggie Smith, a public relations director for Lockheed, in Burbank, California, wanted to see me. I was curious and thought that I should meet her. I was convinced that somebody was playing a joke on me. You see, the last name Rossi is very common in Italy, as common as Smith in English-speaking countries.

Mary Rossi walked in, and my first impression was to say, "Hello, Julie Andrews." Mary looked so much like her! She was the spitting image. I took an immediate liking to Mary, and because I was having a dinner party at the house that evening, I invited Mary and her husband, Theo, to join our friends. She accepted the invitation, and I explained how they could walk to my house through the park.

Come eight p.m., and I suddenly remembered that Luca was not aware of the invitation I had made to Mary and her husband. When I told him, he nearly had a fit. Luca was very formal, and he blurted out, "How could you invite people I don't know? Australians, too!" As if Australians came from some unknown planet.

Finally the doorbell rang and we rushed to the door . . . to find Mary standing there alone.

"Where is your husband?" I asked.

"Oh, we had a fight, so I came alone. He will probably show up later. Sorry I'm late. I started walking through the park and a car followed me. When the guy in the car caught up, he talked to me in Italian, so I couldn't understand. I kept walking and when he caught up with me and started talking to me again, I got so annoyed and scared because it was getting dark. I shrieked, '*Avanti!*' That's one of the half-a-dozen Italian words in my repertoire."

Little did Mary know that "*avanti*" meant "Come on!" No wonder the driver was confused. Mary had been sending mixed signals! The story was so funny, Luca forgot all about his annoyance with me.

Later the Rossis decided to take a sabbatical and come and live in Florence for a few months so that their children could learn Italian. We were still living in Rome, so we often got together. When we moved to Milan, the Rossis still came and visited. In time Mary and Theo had ten kids. In 1975, she was named a member of the Order of the British Empire and in 1978, she was named Mother of the Year in Australia.

Mary and I have now known each other for nearly sixty years, and I was honored to be chosen as godmother to their daughter Danielle, who in 1991 married Christian Helms in York City. The reception was held at Cesarina, the Villa d'Este restaurant in New York City (later called Artusi). Of course I flew over for the occasion, and I was very proud of my goddaughter.

When we moved to Villa d'Este in 1967, Mary came to visit, and she got carried away by the beauty of the lake. She started making plans for me to visit Australia. Mary worked for ten years as the only female TV announcer in Australia. What Mary had in mind was a travel agency; together she and I would introduce the Australians to Villa d'Este. Thanks to Mary, cooking classes at Villa d'Este became the rage among Australians. Soon she arrived with the food expert Leo Schofield and a dozen ladies in tow, all eager to learn how to cook à la Villa d'Este. Beverley Sutherland Smith followed suit, and Villa d'Este became a favorite vacation stopover.

While we are on the subject of food I want to mention Marcella Hazan. I've met her a few times, and of course she is famous in America and a resident of Italy, where she lives with her Italian husband.

One day I was explaining to a friend how Marcella Hazan is unknown in Italy as a chef, and this brings me to discuss how Italians don't use cookbooks. Even though many of the most prominent cookbooks in the world are written by Italians, almost no Italian cook I know owns or uses a cookbook. You see, Italians are expected to know how to cook through some sort of osmosis or natural intuition. Women just don't follow cooking instructions, unless they are those of their mothers or their housekeepers.

But back to my love affair with Australia and the Australians. My first trip to Australia was organized by Mary Rossi, and no better introduction could I have obtained. Whenever I said, "I'm a friend of Mary Rossi," all doors were open to me. In fact, I was so enthused about Australia and the Australians that in the late 1960s I looked into buying a house in the Paddington section of Sydney, an area that at that time was just emerging from being a slum and today is very chic. I fell in love with a freestanding Paddo terrace and I nearly bought it, but then I thought I had better ask Luca if he approved.

He quickly talked me out of my project, "What will I do on Sundays when I cannot watch the ballgame on TV?" That settled it for me.

I was traveling in Australia again in 1970. My plane arrived at Sydney airport at six a.m., and after more than thirty hours in the air, I was completely groggy. Mary Rossi was waiting for me, and without giving me a chance to collect my thoughts, she escorted me to the airport pressroom, which was filled with reporters and photographers waiting to interview and photograph me about Villa d'Este. This had never happened to me before. When I tried to get out of it, Mary said, "Don't be shy; just look at me as if you and I are the only ones in the room." The direction worked, and I have to admit that it was a success, thanks to Mary. After the articles came out in various magazines and newspapers, we had many Australian visitors come for their holidays and vacations at Villa d'Este.

Mary's friend Leo Schofield told Christine Hogan, the journalist, author, editor, and television producer, to look me up. Christine has come regularly every year and has written some great stories about Villa d'Este. Thanks to her, I have met oodles of Australians, like regular guests Elizabeth Rich and Sir Ron Brierley, who visit during the truffle season. Reginald and Kate Johnstone, from Noosa Heads, Queensland, are frequent visitors; and sometimes they even make it twice a year.

But Australia is not my only favorite foreign destination. The other "A," America, has a place in my heart. I think that my family nurtured an early love for the United States; it was instilled by my mother and lasted a lifetime.

It was all thanks to the Fifth Army, which liberated Rome at the end of World War II. Because of them, we were alive. Now my children, Andrea and Claudia, have moved to the U.S.

First it was Claudia, who landed in Key West, Florida, and together with a friend of hers, Antonia Berto, daughter of the Italian author Giuseppe Berto, opened a restaurant—Italian, of course. The novelty was in the fact that it served refined northern Italian cuisine, and the place became popular overnight. Word got around that two attractive girls from Rome were running the restaurant. A frequent customer was playwright Tennessee Williams, who had a regular table.

It took awhile for the locals to discover that the chef, Philip Smith, was not Italian and had never visited Italy. He was a native of Kenosha, Wisconsin, six foot four, blond with blue eyes, and he looked anything but Italian. Claudia and Antonia kept him in the kitchen, taught him to cook and to speak Italian, and before he became too spoiled, Antonia married Philip and they continue to live happily ever after.

I loved going to Key West at Christmas time and having turkey dinner on the beach. I also enjoyed spending January on the island, attending a writers' seminar.

After selling the business, Claudia moved to Chapel Hill, North Carolina, with her husband and children and the Smiths went to Washington, D.C., but they are still the best of friends.

Soon Andrea caught up with Claudia, but he decided that North Carolina was beautiful but not for him. He chose Manhattan because he feels at home where there is hustle and bustle.

Whenever I go to Chapel Hill to visit Claudia and her family, my friend Ellen Sweeney asks me to contact Kristi Yamaguchi, the American figure skater, who for a time lived in Raleigh with her husband, the hockey player Bret Hedican. In her role as head of marketing for the Celanese Corporation, Ellen headed up all sponsorships for the company, and Yamaguchi became the fashion spokesperson for Celanese Acetate. She and Ellen have maintained a long and close friendship, and I am lucky enough to have been brought into it.

I was utterly fascinated to hear Kristi's life history when I first met her. During World War II, her grandparents were sent to an internment camp, in California, where her mother was born. And Kristi's life has not been without hardship either. Kristi began skating as a child as physical therapy for her clubfoot.

She is an amazing woman. She won world championships in figure skating year after year, beginning in 1991. In 2008 Yamaguchi became the celebrity champion in the sixth season of the hit television program *Dancing with the Stars.* She and Bret have two adorable daughters.

In 2000, when they were planning their honeymoon, Ellen Sweeney convinced them that the most romantic place in the world was Lake Como. They took her advice, and I booked them a lovely room with a beautiful view.

I must now turn my attention to one of my favorite subjects: dogs.

Dogs have always had an important role in my life. We have lived through the lives and deaths of many of them, and they have been with Luca and me always, even at the end for Luca.

As I mentioned earlier, after Fido, my first dog who watched over me in my crib, died, my parents immediately replaced him with a purebred

Pekingese who was named Chang Kai-shek. After the demise of Chang Kai-shek in 1939, we returned to Italy. Things were not so bright in Italy, and our family was dogless for those years. We could not really afford to have a pet since we did not have enough food for ourselves, let alone trying to feed another mouth.

Finally the war ended and things started to become normal, and I continued to beg my parents to let me have a dog. Then one day an American soldier brought me a dog in substitution for an engagement ring. I was never to see that soldier again, even though he had made plans to return to Italy after the war and marry me. However, the dog, which I named Bill after him, was with me for a long time. Bill had to be clandestine from my family for a time, but once he was discovered he, like all our other pets, was beloved and became part of the family.

He lived happily for nearly twenty years and stayed with my parents when I traveled.

Years later in 1951, when I joined TWA, I became the godmother of a two-year-old purebred dachshund whose family name was Jasper. He actually belonged to the TWA district sales manager, Carlo Belliero, who was being transferred to London, which meant that Jasper would have had to remain in quarantine for six months. Obviously that was unacceptable, so Jasper became a member of the Salvadore household.

He had a very strong temperament and was attached only to one member of the family—a typical attitude for this breed. The more aristocratic they are, the more conceited they can be. However we got along famously, since I was his chosen one.

I instructed Jasper to sit by Andrea's cradle and watch over him. Jasper seemed to understand that he was not to move unless I permitted him to do so. And, in fact, this job of his was immortalized by my photographer friend Chim in 1952, when he recorded this synergy at our home in Rome, before going across the street to photograph the Bergman-Rossellini twins.

Jasper lived with us for nearly ten years, and he died in my arms.

I was in Australia on a business trip when Luca called to tell me that Jasper was failing rapidly and to be prepared if he passed away before my return. Instead, Jasper waited for me because Luca told him that

I was on my way. When I walked into the house and picked him up, Jasper gave me one last loving look, closed his eyes, and he was gone.

I will not dwell on how upset we all were. Jasper was a member of the family, and he left a void which had to be filled as soon as possible.

Pinky was next. Claudia had a birthday coming up, and this was an occasion to give her a puppy as a gift. We were risking losing our housekeeper, but since it was a birthday present for Claudia, Giulia, the housekeeper, gave in.

The puppy came from a litter of twelve whose mother was a black poodle temporarily stationed in the vet's office at the U.S. Embassy. Claudia named the puppy Pinky because she had just been watching the movie *Pinky* from 1949 starring Jeanne Crain as an ethnically mixed American. The puppy was black except for one white spot on her chest, so my nine-year-old made the leap, and the puppy was named!

Pinky grew up to be the most lovable creature, and she was instantly accepted by the family. She was very smart, as all poodles are.

Along with the vet, we decided not to have her spayed. She did not spend time with other dogs, and she ignored the "birds and the bees" story. We were convinced that she did not seem to miss male dog companionship, and then one day our worst fears were realized.

Luca was walking Pinky in a park when, without warning, she ran off. Luca went after her, but he did not arrive in time because Pinky had already been accosted. She seemed none the worse for wear, and as a matter of fact, she seemed to have had a good time. She was actually smirking!

Notwithstanding her advanced age—Pinky was nearly ten years old—we called the vet when Pinky started acting strangely soon after her tryst in the park. We were convinced that she was pregnant, but the vet was sure that it was a hysterical (false) pregnancy.

Two months passed, and one night we heard her whimpering. She had her little bed in our bedroom, so Luca and I were able to quickly run to attend her needs. It didn't take us long to realize that she was having labor pains. I immediately called the vet, who confirmed what he had already told us: Pinky was having an hysterical pregnancy and she was going through all the various stages as if it was a normal delivery.

Our darling Pinky looked up at me with big soulful eyes, and I promised her I would help. Luca disappeared because he could not bear to see our beloved Pinky suffer. In no time, two beautiful little puppies popped out, but they were dead. Pinky licked them clean and I took them away, planning to bury them. Then we all three, Luca, Pinky, and I, settled down and managed to rest for a while.

A couple of hours later I opened my eyes to find Pinky delivering one puppy after another. There were three in all, and very much alive. We congratulated Pinky, and once again we went to sleep.

For the next couple of months I took care of Pinky and her puppies until we were able to give the little ones away. I found homes for them, and finally Pinky, who lacked maternal instincts, was quite relieved when she saw them go.

After Pinky died of old age, we hesitated to get another pet because it had been heartrending when she left us. We decided not to add another pet to our family, but fate was against us, for soon Pinky's place was taken by Max. A dear friend of ours, Countess Stucchi of Cernobbio, called to ask if we would like to adopt a puppy whose mother came from the Caribbean islands. The countess, a real animal lover, had been on a holiday in Antigua, and she had been picked up by a lovely stray dog that roamed the beaches. When my friend asked the hotel manager who would take care of the dog once she left, he answered, "You have spoiled her so much, the only thing to do is to have her put down."

The countess was horrified, and on the spur of the moment she decided to take the dog with her back to Italy.

Well, it wasn't that easy. There were so many documents and lots of red tape. To make a long story short, she made it home (meaning Lake Como), and after a few weeks the dog gave birth to eight puppies, and that is how I got one. We knew the mother, but we had no idea who the father was.

Since we were able to choose, I decided our puppy had to be a male, and my heart went out to one golden-colored puppy. Then we had to find a name, and we immediately decided on a rather pompous one: Maximilian d'Este.

After all, Villa d'Este was to become his home and although he was just a mutt we never let him know. We called him Max for short. He grew up to be such a handsome fellow. He looked like a cross between a Golden Retriever and a Labrador Retriever. People would stop Luca and ask him what breed Max was, and my husband would reply, "A Salvadore." This made Max happy because, let us face it, he was very vain. He led a long, healthy life and he died serenely only a few days before I left for New York to launch *Villa d'Este Style.* I am convinced that he knew I would not have left if he was still alive.

My Max was beloved by all. He was the last pet I had, and everybody still remembers him. He died in 2000. My favorite snapshot of Max is the one in front of the famous Villa d'Este mosaic, where Max appears to be walking me. He is really tugging and I am having trouble keeping up with him. Also in the photo, seen from the back, is Edward De Luca, whose New York art gallery DC Moore is an attraction for all art lovers. Edward is trying to snap Max and me on this "person" walk. At the same time my darling friend Steven Kaufmann was photographing the whole scene.

Max loved walking around the Villa d'Este park, and whenever possible he would run off and climb up the hill and look down on the lake, the floating swimming pool, barely visible in the picture, and our house, which is not visible in the photo, but Max knew where to look.

No dog could take his place

A few years ago, Andrea did something that made me cry: He commissioned a well-known artist to do an oil portrait of Max. Today that painting hangs over my mantelpiece.

This time, I really mean it. No more dogs.

But I still have three dreams: The first is that when I "grow up," I want to live in the country, and I couldn't find a better place than my mosaic hideaway in the park of Villa d'Este. The second is that I want to be surrounded by books, and those I have in abundance. And the third is that I would like to have a dog to keep me company. However, I have to remind myself that I am having trouble taking care of myself, let alone a pet!

I've even had dog attachments to dogs not living with me, over the years. In 1980, word was out that I had bought property on the island of Elba, for love of Arturo. (Luca and I had actually purchased the property in 1974.) Who was Arturo? Arturo was a dog. He was a purebred hunting hound, but when he grew old his owner, having no use for him anymore, drove to Poggio (the village on Elba where we had our house) and abandoned him there. The villagers didn't care two hoots about the poor dog. They called him Arturo because he resembled a workman who did a lot of odd jobs for everybody in the village.

I befriended Arturo (the dog, not the workman) and made him sleep in my house and, of course, I fed him. It was the butcher who informed me that Arturo had another godmother who really took care of him. Her name was Betty Hogg and she had a house next to mine. Her husband was the Hogg of the giant corporate travel services company Hogg Robinson, so she always arrived on the island in a private helicopter. She liked to come off season, while I always tried to be on the island in full summer.

Between the two of us, Arturo was well attended. I opened up an account with the local butcher, and I taught Arturo to show up there every day to have a meal so that he would be "covered" even when Mrs. Hogg and I were not on the island. When I returned to Poggio, I went to pay my debt, and the butcher informed me that Arturo had been showing up with a retinue of his friends—the other stray dogs of Elba.

I informed Betty, and she said, "I'll take care of it."

She loaded the helicopter with canned dog meat and brought it to Elba so that Arturo and his friends had enough food to last a lifetime.

Here is an excerpt from a letter from Betty.

I don't have to tell you how frightful I felt at leaving Arturo, but at least he is so much better, you would not recognize him. I spent hours and hours with him and think he MAY have forgotten his ghastly experience.

His legs are far better and many in the village thanked me for helping him. I also informed all who would listen that there was absolutely NO reason for him to be put to sleep so far as his legs were concerned. He is a bit lame but so much better and I said just because Mr. Hogg was very lame, I had no intention of putting HIM to sleep—therefore no necessity for Arturo.

Elba is not well known except for the fact that Napoleon was exiled here. When one of his lady friends, Countess Marie Waleska, arrived on Elba, where did they meet? In Poggio, my village!

The year 1998 didn't look as if anything sensational was about to happen; instead we purchased a Hotel outside Florence, which was advertised on Internet. Without wasting any time, Jean-Marc Droulers rounded up some of the staff, starting with Claudio Ceccherelli, then general manager of Villa d'Este, and other members of the staff, including myself. When we arrived at Villa la Massa, we were utterly speechless because we knew immediately that this property was exactly what we were looking for. Built in 1525, it became a five-star Villa as described by Clive Irving in a great story he wrote for *Condé Nast Traveler.*

The years 2001 and 2002 were my *annus horribilis.* The worst day was September 11th, the day when New York's World Trade Center towers were attacked by terrorists and thousands died. The attack took place around three p.m. our time, and I happened to be at home and on my way back to the hotel when Andrea called from New York, telling me to turn on the TV. When I saw what was happening I rushed to the hotel and told the guests what was happening. Many wanted to leave right away, but it was impossible to contact the airlines and all the airports were closed.

My son Andrea, who is a documentary film producer, made a film on this tragic event. It was shown on Italian television a few days after it happened.

I did not return to New York until January 2002, in time for the memorial service of Jane Montant, editor of *Gourmet* magazine. That year also counted the memorial service for Beni Montresor, the Italian artist who was a set designer and children's book illustrator, who passed away in October 2001.

It was also the year 2002, when I started falling apart physically, needing one operation after the other, replacements of knees and hips. Then I had a battle with cancer. Happily, my treatment went well and I am a survivor. I had almost forgotten that I had already had cancer and survived, because that was during the time that Luca became ill and died. That overshadowed everything else back in 1986.

In December 1986, when Luca was treated for cancer—a word that was never spoken aloud—I was so completely taken by surprise that I reacted in a strange way because I refused to accept the doctor's words. I just could not believe that my Luca, who at his worst suffered a cold once in a blue moon, had been diagnosed as having a tumor. Of course we had to wait for the results of the biopsy to find out if it was malignant, but the look on the surgeon's face had me worried. It was like a nightmare, a very bad dream from which I would wake up and everything would go back to normal. Wishful thinking!

Christmas was coming up, and the surgeon asked if we would prefer to have Luca's surgery before or after the holiday. We decided that if it had to be done, the sooner the better, upon which the surgeon had Luca hospitalized. He explained that if the operation lasted only a couple of hours, it meant that it was too late to hope for a recovery; but if it lasted over five hours, then there were good chances of recovery. The operation lasted nearly seven hours . . . whoopie! We (my son, daughter, and I) were ready to celebrate Christmas, but poor Luca was not up to it.

Christmas Day came, and we were only allowed to spend a couple of hours with our beloved one because he was in the post-operation ward. He was being well looked after. It took awhile, but little by little Luca seemed to be getting better and gaining his strength back.

Luca made a wonderful comeback, and we decided that I would accompany him at the end of the season on a tour of the United States, drumming up business for Villa d'Este. We traveled from the East Coast to the West Coast, with stopovers in Texas, where Luca was visited by some of the best specialists on his condition. They didn't give me much hope. He slowly started failing.

By the time we returned to Italy from our last trip in 1987, I don't think Luca was aware that he had little time to live because he was not in pain. He died in his bed at home with his son, daughter, and me at his bedside, along with my close friend and colleague Annamaria Duvia, who is always included in our family. And of course our Max was there, our beloved doggie who never left Luca's side during those last days.

It was touching to see how Max was devoted to his master Luca. We brought Luca home so that we could give him our loving care and be with him all the time. This would not have been possible in the hospital, where visits were limited to a couple of hours each day.

There was absolutely no hope for him to recover, and he did not want to remain in the hospital. When we brought him home for the last time, Max was beside himself with joy. But he understood immediately that Luca was unable to play around so, once his master had settled down under the blankets, Max put his head on the cushion next to Luca and refused to budge.

Every morning our doctor would stop by and Max would look at him suspiciously, so Dr. Moltrasio would reassure him.

Luca was very tired and tried to sleep as much as possible. He was having some bad dreams and would scream, "Take me home!" He would calm down once we convinced him that he was in his bed at home. We told him that he could not be in the hospital because dogs were not allowed.

The doctor always came and would shake his head, and talking to Max, he would say, "Max, I'm doing my best." Max wanted to believe him. This went on for a few days until the fatal hour arrived. My children were present and of course Max, too.

The doctor arrived, and all he could do was prepare the death certificate. As the doctor got up from the chair and started walking to the door, Max went after him and took a nip on his behind, tearing his pants.

I was so flabbergasted and was about to scold Max when the doctor said, "It's my fault. I was unable to help his master."

But enough about all the illness and disaster. How about some remembrances of the superstars who have found their way to Villa d'Este, just in the years that I have been here? Of those there have been plenty.

For five consecutive years beginning in June 1988, Villa d'Este hosted movie stars from the 1940s in a special event known as Viva Hollywood. It created quite a stir in the sleepy villages surrounding Lake Como. It wasn't every day that the locals, never mind the visitors to the hotel, were able to bump into Bette Davis, June Allyson trailing behind Gene Kelly, Robert Mitchum, Joseph Cotten, or Glenn Ford, as they were during this time at the hotel. And even some younger actresses like Samantha Eggar and Ali MacGraw were occasionally in attendance. Each year, eight celebrities were invited to spend a week vacationing on Lake Como and enjoying the beautiful panoramic surroundings. At the end of their stay, a gala dinner was held in the casino of Campione d'Italia in Switzerland, less than half an hour from Villa d'Este.

The first event, in 1988, celebrated the sixtieth anniversary of the Academy Awards. It was quite a sight to see all these great stars roaming the back streets of Cernobbio. I was especially impressed by Bette Davis, who always called for me when she needed something. She complimented me by saying that I spoke the most beautiful English. I was so flattered that I was at her beck and call throughout her stay. She was so tiny and weak, having undergone three major operations, but she nonetheless took over and ran the show.

We had organized a press conference in the Villa d'Este theatre, but Miss D (as I was authorized to call her) refused to appear with her fellow actors and actresses. The press conference was to be held for her alone! I was completely mesmerized by her, as was everybody else in the room, including the members of the press. I never thought she would make it to her conference. But she asked me to give her a few minutes, and refusing my assistance, she managed to get up and walk behind the armchair.

She pulled herself together, and suddenly she looked about six feet tall. She lit a cigarette and smoked throughout the press conference. As always, she put on a great performance. I spent a lot of time with her and enjoyed every minute of it because she was a most interesting woman, and I wept when she left. She left me with the sage advice that a happy marriage is the result of "one bed and two bathrooms." I heartily agree. Sadly, she died at her home only a few weeks later.

In 1989 the group consisted of Joan Fontaine, Kim Novak, Rod Steiger, Jean Simmons, Kirk Douglas, Anthony Perkins, Cliff Robertson, and Jane Russell.

But before I finish up on my tales of Viva Hollywood at Villa d'Este, I must tell a story about Robert Mitchum. He was even better looking in person than any character he ever portrayed in a film. He had a look that said it all—his glance told you that he didn't care one way or the other about anything.

While he and his wife were visiting Villa d'Este in June of 1988, I got to know his wife, Dorothy, who struck me as a real lady.

I mentioned to my son Andrea that Robert Mitchum was staying at Villa d'Este, and Andrea exclaimed, "Mother, I must have his autograph. Didn't you know that he is my favorite actor?"

"No way," I retorted. "I can't go around asking for autographs. I'm too old to behave like a teenage fan!"

My Andrea seemed so disappointed that I added, "I'll try." He was thirty-five years old, but he was still my little boy. And I *was* spending the evening with Robert and Dorothy.

Mitchum was pacing up and down the room, so I took advantage of his absence to ask Dorothy if she could help me get an autograph from her husband. She called him over, "Will you please stop walking up and down and listen to Jean, who has a favor to ask?"

Because I hesitated, Dorothy stepped in and said, "Jean's son thinks you are a great actor and wishes to have your autograph."

"How old is he?" asked Mitchum.

When I said, "Thirty-five," he said, "Oh, fine. Is he married?"

"No."

"Would he consider asking my daughter to marry him? If so, I will give him a photo complete with the autograph."

He was joking, of course! My son got what he wanted without having to marry Mitchum's daughter. We never got them together.

And then there was Douglas Fairbanks, Jr., the handsome son of the swashbuckling silent film star Douglas Fairbanks. Junior arrived one day at Villa d'Este—without a reservation. We were happy to accommodate him. He was definitely a very debonair gentleman. Fairbanks seemed to be in a friendly mood, so I asked him, "What brought you to Villa d'Este?"

"When I was a little boy I came here with my father," he replied. "Then, a few days ago I picked up a copy of *Town and Country* magazine. There was a great story about Lake Como, in which Villa d'Este was prominently featured. I decided on the spur of the moment to fly over and see for myself if the hotel really is as beautiful as described. You want to know something? It's even better!"

Renato Guttuso, the Italian painter, a friend of Pablo Picasso, was considered the number one artist in Italy after the Second World War. Of Sicilian origin, Guttuso grew up in the so-called "mafia" region. A true communist, he donated half his earnings to the party. He married a very rich lady from Varese, not far from Villa d'Este, and often spent weekends at the hotel. Luca and I got to know them, and it didn't take long to strike up a friendship.

When Guttuso found out that my Luca was half Sicilian (Luca's father came from Taormina, close to Messina), he would go out of his way to make him happy. He was ready to adopt my Luca because he did not have any children of his own and he considered Luca a true Sicilian. Every time we dined together, he taught me some typical Sicilian dish. Our favorite was peppers filled with little penne, baked in the oven.

In return, when Renato and his wife Mimise came to our place, I would make a risotto.

One evening at my house I plucked up my courage, and I asked Renato if he would recognize a drawing signed by him. I wanted to be sure that it was an original drawing. The drawing showed a woman's derriere. When he saw it, he said to Mimise, "Whose ass is that?"

Mimise, in a very dignified tone of voice, answered, "It is mine, of course."

With that, he asked for paper and pencil and drew a naked woman, very discreet, which of course I framed. It hangs next to Mimise's ass!

I Promessi Sposi (The Betrothed) is a book written by one of Italy's great novelists, Alessandro Manzoni. The story takes place on Lake Como, and it is about a young couple who intend to marry, but the ceremony is much delayed by unexpected obstacles. The book is a mainstay of Italian literature, studied in classrooms all over the country.

Villa d'Este has had its fair share of "betrotheds," and many of those have come from stage and screen. Just recently, Brad Pitt and Angelina Jolie visited, seemingly in search of a matrimonial spot. The paparazzi decided that they had chosen Villa d'Este, which had just reopened its gates for the 2006 season. The story overtook the papers and television; it was as though the world had come to a standstill because the only interest was in the potential nuptials of the century.

Villa d'Este was under siege, not only by the paparazzi but also by the legitimate press, many of whom came from Hollywood and booked themselves into the hotel. They wouldn't believe me when I repeatedly told them that Brad and Angelina never made a booking. They got in touch with the couple's friend George Clooney, who happens to have a villa next door to Villa d'Este. The interest then centered on the Clooney villa. Surely "il bel Giorgio" (the handsome George) knew the whereabouts of the couple and their wedding site, as well.

The local papers even published the dates—sometime between March 12th and 18th in 2006. And what's more, the mayor of Cernobbio, Simona Saladini, held a press conference to announce the fact! She was photographed in a "Lucia," a rowboat typical of Lake Como, which had been purchased by City Hall because the mayor planned to marry the couple in the boat, and for the occasion she had a pale blue outfit made. Of course Brad and Angelina never showed up, but on the other hand they never had made a booking, so it may be that I alone was not surprised by this turn of events!

Years have now passed, and the two are still not married. Well, we shall see, but it's likely that a spot like Villa d'Este, which has security, seclusion, and a unique ambience, would be a reasonable choice of location for a wedding.

Later we received a real request for a wedding at Villa d'Este. This time it was Tom Cruise and his bride-to-be, Katie Holmes. I remember coming through the bar one evening and seeing a lovely young woman, whom I must admit I did not recognize in the least, sitting at the bar. I asked Ilio, our barman who knew everybody, and everybody knew Ilio, who she was, and he reported it was Katie Holmes *sans* Tom Cruise, who would join her later.

They were quite serious about having their wedding at Villa d'Este, because Katie really "cased the joint," as one says—but it would not work out. They wanted to take over the hotel, and we were forced to turn down their request because we had guests arriving during the dates they requested; in fact, the hotel was completely sold out.

I'm sure she was taken with Villa d'Este. However, taking over the entire hotel was impossible; we are almost never in a position to allow it because we are usually "under siege" by our regular guests and visitors.

Eventually we read in the papers that Katie and Tom had a wedding at the Castello di Bracciano near Rome, and caused near riots in the streets when they did. There wasn't much seclusion to that event, as it turned out.

Years ago when my Australian friend Eve Harman, editor-in-chief of *Vogue* for thirty years, would stop off at Villa d'Este with her daughter and my godchild Samantha, I told Sammy that when she grew up and found a husband I wanted her to get married at the hotel. Time went by, and one day Sammy called me to say that she had a future husband in tow and they were ready to come to Lake Como and get married. She and Anthony and about forty-eight relatives and friends showed up, and it was a beautiful ceremony. So beautiful that it bought tears to our eyes!

As you know by now, some of my best and most longstanding friends, both at TWA and Villa d'Este, are from the artistic community, especially photographers, writers, and fashionistas. "One picture is worth a thousand words," goes the timeworn saying. But how many photographers are aware that photography was invented on Lake Como?

For more than two thousand years, poets from Virgil and Catullus to Tennyson and Longfellow have raved about the lakes of the Lombardy region, but it is impossible to do justice to the spectacular beauty of Lake Como without a photograph. The beauty of the lake inspired the English scientist William Fox Talbot to imprint images of the extraordinary Lake Como on paper. He visited Como in October 1833, and upon returning to England in January 1834, he went to work in his laboratory. The memory of Como's beauty drove him on, as did the knowledge that the Frenchman Louis Daguerre was working toward the same goal: the invention of photography. The two men today share the distinction of having invented photography, but Como shares with no other locale the honor of having inspired it.

When I was a child, I decided that when I grew up I would become a photographer. Unfortunately I never made the grade, but I was always watching for photographers. I enjoyed trailing after them when they came to Villa d'Este to do a shoot, whether it was fashion, food, or scenery. I learned to love Lake Como through the lens of some of the greatest photographers.

This is how I came to know some of the most famous photographers, starting from the end of the war to today. I did get to know quite a few. For instance, there was Slim Aarons, who was noted for photographing café society and, later, jet-setters.

Slim became a celebrity, and he thoroughly enjoyed mixing with the "beautiful people" because he was one of them. At age 18 Aarons enlisted in the U.S. Army and became a combat photographer in World War II, where he even earned a Purple Heart. After the war, he traveled from one continent to another and from one party to another, beautifully recording what he saw.

We met in Rome after the Allies had made their triumphal entry into the Eternal City. Slim dropped in at the canteen where I distributed doughnuts to the troops. We met, we chatted, and for thirty years we lost contact. Finally, in the late 1960s, Slim returned to do a special issue on Italy for *Holiday* magazine. It appeared in 1970.

Come 1984, and Slim was sent on assignment by *Town and Country* magazine to do a story on the hotel. I made appointments for Slim to take photos, and the first stop was Gianni Versace's villa. The great designer kept us waiting for more than an hour although I had made an appointment and explained the purpose of our visit. Gianni did not blink an eye or offer us an apology, so I just walked out, but Slim stayed on because the shoot without a photo of Gianni Versace would not be complete. After all, he was at his prime and it would have been unforgiveable to ignore him, notwithstanding his bad manners.

From Villa Fontanelle, Versace's villa, we proceeded to other villas such as the Villa Arconati at the Balbianello, which belonged to Count Guido Monzino. The count gave us a royal welcome and made us stay for lunch. It was a pleasure to visit this villa, considered the most beautiful in the area. The only disappointment was that Monzino refused to don sports attire while he rowed in a little boat—he wore his double-breasted gray suit.

Everybody knows Annie Leibovitz, partly because of the photo she took of John Lennon and Yoko Ono on the day he was killed. She came to do a photo story on Lake Como, George Clooney, and of course, Villa d'Este. The hotel was her home base during the shoot.

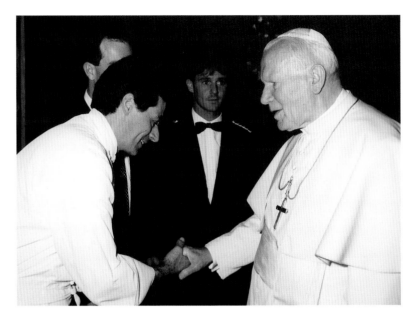

The Pope, (John Paul II) came to Lake Como in 1996 and chef Luciano Parolari had planned to serve him a meal of chicken with broth. But the Pope declined: he wanted some of Luciano's famous risotto, so the menu was revised.

Carla Porta Musa was invited to the first Chef's Table, instituted at Villa d'Este in 1995, after a visit to New York for a dinner at the United Nations, which held a similar event.

Also atending this inaugural Chef's Table are *(clockwise)* President/CEO Jean-Marc Droulers, Carla Porta Musa, the author, Annamaria Duvia, Public Relations Manager, and Raffaela Bruni, wife of the Mayor of Como.

The "Kitchen Brigade" of chefs that cook in Parolari's kitchens for the hotel's restaurants, Veranda and Grill.

A first trip to America was to offer an Italian cooking class to a limited clientele at the behest of Sissie and Billy Morris of Augusta, Georgia. This photo includes the author, Parolari, and Billy Morris.

Chef Parolari poses in his "kitchen garden" which forms the basis for all the seasonal dishes served on the menu at Villa d'Este.

Following: Once Villa d'Este established itself as a center of fine Italian cuisine, cooking classes became the rage. This one, organized by travel agent Barbara Fouhy *(far right)*, was for Americans.

Bill *(above)* and Jasper *(right)* were the author's dogs in Rome. Jasper, as previously mentioned, served as a watchdog over the bassinets of the author's children Andrea and Claudia.

Above: Arturo, the author's adopted dog on the island of Elba, found that although he started as a stray, he had more "owners" and friends than most dogs—and ate better than most humans, to boot.

Right: Pinky was the Salvadore family companion in Milan and seemed to have made the transition to living at Villa d'Este without issue.

Buffo, above, lived very well at Villa d'Este until he lost his hearing. He was the author's first dog at the hotel.

Max was the author's most beloved dog, and also a Villa d'Este resident, re-membered with great affection by many of the author's friends and family.

Distinguished and blessed with a very distinctive personality, Max took charge of his environment. The author always said that Max walked her rather than the reverse.

The party to celebrate the 125th birthday of the hotel was held on July 28, 1998. Cocktails were served lakeside followed by a grand dinner in the Emprie room, finishing with fireworks over the lake. *Left:* Jean-Marc Droulers and his son, Francois, pour champagne; and *right:* the extraordinary fireworks display.

The delicious and elegant anniversary cake prepared by Luciano Parolari and his staff.

Guests and friends of the hotel arrived from all parts of the world to celebrate the birthday event.

The author with good friend and bestselling author, Bill Wright.

Joseph Heller, here with the author at the foyer to the Veranda restaurant at the hotel, generously wrote the foreword to the author's book, *Villa d'Este Style*, and it was his last written work before his death.

Author David Leavitt and Valerie Humphries Heller, wife of Joseph Heller, enjoy a lunchtime get-together on the famed Veranda's lakeside terrace.

Bill Blass confidante and best friend of the author, Steven Kaufmann began every week in New York with a phone call to the author at Villa d'Este. Here he is lakeside (both), his favorite spot at the hotel.

American editor and colleague who became as close as family, Pamela Fiori and husband Colt Givner are frequent visitors to Italy and in particular, to visit Jean Salvadore at Villa d'Este.

The cake for the author's 80th birthday was an elaborate and delicious extravaganza presented to Jean by chef Luciano Parolari *(to the right of the author)* and his first assistant, Angelo Bosetti *(far left)*, and pastry chef, Yuri *(far right)*.

As Jean Salvadore's favorite color is red, all of the decorations at her birthday celebration were that color.

Fashion designer Beppe Spadaccini is one of Como's most esteemed artists and a close and long-term friend of the author.

Other birthday guests include, from left to right, Pietro Zendali *(standing)*, Dr. Jim Bonorris *(seated)* with his wife Lucy *(standing behind)*, next to Edward De Luca *(also standing)* and, seated to the right, journalist Giuseppe Guin and his wife, Silvia.

The author at her home on the Villa d'Este premises, known as the "hole in the wall," with her daughter Claudia and son Andrea.

Andrea Salvadore with Tommy, Martina, and wife Christina in their
New York apartment.

Claudia Salvadore with her sons Luca *(center)* and Patrick at their home
in North Carolina.

Opening day festivities in March 2010 with Jean-Marc Droulers *(left)* with the unfurled Villa d'Este flag and Droulers *(right)* with hotel manager Danilo Zuchetti.

Following: A rare snowfall blankets the famous mosaics of Villa d'Este.

Luca's tree on the grounds of Villa d'Este.

A funny episode: The day before leaving, she joined some of the hotel management staff for lunch. Once we were all seated, she decided to take a photo of our president and CEO, Jean-Marc Droulers; the general manager, Danilo Zucchetti; and myself.

Annie Leibovitz taught me how to look natural and not posed. Then she reached for her camera, which she kept in a big duffel bag, glanced at it with a perplexed expression on her face, and blurted out, "I don't know how to use it!"

To say that we were shocked by such a statement coming from Annie is putting it mildly. She explained that she always has one of her assistants at her side, who prepares the camera so all she has to do is click. Unfortunately, this story explains how I was not photographed by Annie Leibovitz! But she was so nice to send me her latest book with a lovely inscription.

There are various categories of photographers, but Ronny Jaques was in a class of his own. In October 2008 I flew to New York to attend the launch of the book *Stolen Moments: The Photographs of Ronny Jaques,* authored by *Town and Country* editor Pamela Fiori. This is an important book because Ronny was really one of the greats; but he was very self-effacing and never made a show of himself or his work. Because of this, he has been largely ignored, but those of us like Pamela and me, who worked with Ronny, remember him with reverence both as a talent and as a person.

Ronny was a very solitary artist, who worked only with his camera, film, and a few lenses. No assistants, no minions, no demands. He just immersed himself in his assignment and created beautiful artwork from it. And he wasn't just a photographer for commerce; he was also an art photographer who created incredible photographs of children running in Ireland and landscapes in Italy, all in black and white.

I remember when on various occasions, Ronny accompanied Jane Montant from *Gourmet* magazine to Villa d'Este to shoot food from our kitchen. This was *Gourmet*'s first visit to the hotel, and it took place more than thirty years ago. The night of their arrival we—Jane, Ronny, Luca, and I—dined together and made plans for Ronny to take photos the next day. We would meet for breakfast and further our plans.

The next morning Jane, Luca, and I went ahead and had breakfast because obviously Ronny had overslept. When he joined us and announced that he had taken all the photos that were needed for the story and we could all sit back and enjoy life at the villa. One of the photos made the cover of *Gourmet*. Jane and I resumed our embroidery, and we had the best time exploring all the small, delightfully picturesque villages along the waterfront of Lake Como together.

Helmut Newton's visit to Villa d'Este and my interactions with him have been published many times and are among my most extraordinary ever. Newton wrote in his autobiography, "Villa d'Este is a place with the most sensuous surroundings and fascinating history," and he knows because he helped to enhance its reputation for sensuousness. I now think it's a funny story, but at the time, in the early 1970s, it upset me no end.

At the beginning of the year 1973, I believe, I received a call from a friend of the great photographer Helmut Newton, explaining that Newton had expressed a wish to do a shoot at Villa d'Este, something that had been his childhood dream. I very politely said that I could not grant permission because I was familiar with his work, which I didn't think would improve the hotel's image.

Soon the friend called back to confide in me. Newton was a very sick man and would not be living long. Being a sentimental fool, I fell for this sad story (by the way, Newton lived many years after that conversation, until 2004). I reluctantly gave permission, with one stipulation: that the photos had to be seen and approved by Villa d'Este before they were published by the French magazine *Réalités,* for which Newton was on assignment.

Newton arrived with his two gorgeous models. I stayed with them throughout the shoot, and later the hotel was sent a printed copy of the magazine. Everything was in order. What a relief.

A few months passed and I happened to be in New York when a photographer friend, Franny Gill, called to invite me to the launch of Helmut Newton's new book, *White Women.* The hall was crowded, and Newton did a great job explaining how he had managed to shoot a second set of "erotic" photos at Villa d'Este when on the shoot for *Réalités.* Apparently when I had left the room to get him a cup of tea, as he had requested, he'd asked his models to lower their dresses, and so he made a second set of Villa d'Este photographs.

Naturally, I was mortified—and also worried about how this might affect my long-term standing with the directors of the hotel, who were a group of very elegant and reserved Italian men. Not wanting Newton to see me at the book launch, I sneaked out with a copy of the book and made my way back to Villa d'Este, feeling very unhappy with myself. How could I have let Helmut Newton make such a fool of me? I decided that the only thing to do was to come clean with the hotel board of directors and to call it quits. I prepared my letter of resignation to present to the members.

When I appeared before them, shame-faced and holding the book, the board members grabbed it and passed it around in silence. I was congratulated for my "coup" and handed a new contract. Who knew the power of seminaked women posed at the best hotel in the world?

Jean-Marc Droulers reminded me that Helmut Newton, who died in 2004, participated to the "Concorso d'Eleganza Villa d'Este" in the year 2002. The Concorso d'Eleganza, the automotive beauty contest, takes place at Villa d'Este every year in April and Jean-Marc Droulers adds that Villa d'Este offers an atmosphere you will not find elsewhere. How true! The Concorso is one of the world's top classic car events. I love to watch the parade of vintage cars that brings you back to the 1920s.

Red is my favorite color, and I do have a "designer" story about this. In 2009, I was in New York for a few days and when I called my friend Ellen Sweeney, she invited me to a party given by her friend, Clodagh, in her 12,000-square-foot studio in Manhattan's Soho. Irish-born Clodagh was celebrating her twenty-fifth anniversary of design in New York, creating everything from makeup packaging to million-square-foot hotels.

Clodagh had written a couple of books with her husband, photographer Daniel Aubry, and I was really looking forward to meeting this artist, who sounded absolutely fascinating. So I got myself all done up, and I decided to wear a red Valentino that I had bought on sale years earlier. It's a classic: very simple and easily recognizable as a Valentino because of its Valentino trademark buttons.

I went off with Ellen to Clodagh's loft with nary a care in the world, to find that dozens of people were gathering. By the end of the evening, a few hundred had arrived. Did I mention my surprise when I realized that I was the *only person*—male or female—NOT dressed in black? Women wore slacks, dresses, ensembles, all black from head to toe; and the men were similarly in black trousers paired with black shirts, turtlenecks, sweaters. I probably don't need to tell you that in my red Valentino I stuck out like a sore thumb. To say that I was embarrassed is putting it mildly; nevertheless, it turned out to be an extremely enjoyable evening.

My favorite designer is still Bill Blass. We met in New York through mutual friends and at IdeaComo, the biannual textile show at Villa d'Este. IdeaComo is an invasion of the international fashion set, who come intent on finding the latest in quality silks, cottons, linens, and synthetics. Textile manufacturing in Como stems back to 1550, and the region today is renowned as a leader in producing silk.

Blass was often in attendance, and frequently the guest of honor as well. When IdeaComo was first held at Villa d'Este, some thirty years ago, Bill Blass wrote, "There is no doubt about it. The wonderful ambiance of Villa d'Este makes it the number one place to visit for a most fashionable clientele."

I met "Bilbo," as his most intimate friends called him, through mutual friends, one of whom was my dearest friend, Steven Kaufmann, who died in 2004. Steven's *New York Times* obituary was titled, "The Death of an Unknown Man Who Knew Everyone," and this was surely the case with Steven, who seemed to know everyone, everywhere, although he himself was not famous. I was mentioned in the obituary because every Monday Steven would call me, and we kept this up until he died. Whenever I went to New York, the first person I would contact was Steven.

His family owned the Kaufmann department store chain in Pittsburgh, so Steven grew up in the fashion industry. After World War II, Stevie, as his friends called him, moved to New York permanently. When he was seventy, Bill Blass offered Steven a job, and the rest was history. Although Steven started working late in life, he seemed to enjoy it.

I met him for the first time in 1951, when I was with TWA and Stevie was traveling with Jerry Zipkin (who later served as Nancy Reagan's frequent escort). Howard Hughes's office advised me to take good care of them.

Steven and I clicked immediately, as did Luca and even my children. Claudia, at the age of twenty-two, still called Steven uncle and would try to wrangle lunch invitations out of him while she was in New York to brush up on her English.

Claudia survived by wrapping packages at Christmas at Bloomingdales and he promised to feed her as long as she didn't show up in jeans! Stevie visited with us once a year, following us around from Rome to Fregene, to Milan and Villa d'Este.

Bill Blass was the first designer to ignore the backrooms of Seventh Avenue and be welcomed into the chic Manhattan drawing rooms. Bill put his name on a variety of products, from blue jeans and bed linens to automobiles. One year during IdeaComo, he called me up and said he was coming over and would I cook for him? Of course! I was honored!

I loved the guy, and I declare Bill was the most handsome man in town. He always had a cigarette in his mouth, and I sometimes wonder how he would have managed today when you cannot even smoke in your own home. Then I found out why he wanted to catch me away from the crowds.

"Are you still using the perfume Joy?" he asked me one day. "Well, you will not wear it any longer. From now on your perfume will be Bill Blass."

This happened over thirty years ago, and I am still using Bilbo's perfume or, better still, the eau de cologne. People recognize me from my perfume, and I still have a good supply, which was given to me before Blass died.

On another subject: One of my favorite pastimes is to browse around a small bookstore where the owner is a friend—he certainly greets me like one. As soon as he sees me he says, "I have a book for you that you are going to love."

He gets the book. It is *Madame Solario.* On the pastel-colored cover there is a lady dressed in the fashion of the eighteenth century. In the background, there is a typical view of a lake village. The subtitle reads, "The famous anonymous novel of passion and decadence."

I couldn't wait to start reading the book, which, of course, takes place on Lake Como. It is about a group of friends who are spending a holiday in the fashionable resort of Cadenabbia on Lake Como.

One gentleman, a Russian, is trying to purchase Villa Balbianello. The mysterious Madame Solario and others enjoy a quiet life on the shores of Tremezzo-Cadenabbia. On Saturday evenings, the only place for a chic outing is Villa d'Este—a journey that was quite an adventure when done by horse and buggy. The Villa d'Este was a real swinging place; guests would arrive from all parts of the world.

One of my favorite writers is David Leavitt, who is a visitor to the hotel. How did I get to know David Leavitt? As already mentioned, I've always tried to keep abreast of what is going on in the cultural world. A new book comes out and I look at all the reviews to decide whether I want to read it.

One day in 1997, I was in the office (the back room, as I call it) when an agent from the reception desk asked me if I had any material available on the hotel for a guest who had just arrived.

I collected all I could and went out to meet the gentleman. Surprise!

"Hello, David Leavitt," I said.

"How do you know me?" he asked.

"I've seen your photo and I've read your books."

Later I found out that David was staying incognito at Villa d'Este because he was writing an article about the hotel for *Travel and Leisure*.

So that is how it all started. We became friends and I got to know his companion, Mark Mitchell, and their dog, Tolo. They were living in Tuscany, but now they are in Florida and David teaches at the University of Florida.

An excerpt from his story, which I particularly enjoyed:

Wherever we turn, there are children: tearing along the patio, or playing with a Dalmatian puppy in the garden, or splashing in the swimming pool that floats on the lake. Their vivid presence surprises me; I had expected the Villa d'Este to be stuffier than this, a place where you have to keep your voice down. But rarely have I seen ease and formality so happily married. A waiter flirts with a curly headed little girl; the maitre d' opens his photo album to reveal snapshots of his Harley-Davidson and the pope; under the statue of Venus (attributed to Canova), a child begs her mother for a Barbie.

Another visitor known for her writing, among other talents, is Kathleen Kennedy Townsend, the eldest of Robert and Ethel Kennedy's children and the oldest grandchild of Joseph P. and Rose Kennedy.

Kathleen was invited by the European House Ambrosetti Forum, which holds its meetings once a year, early each September at Villa d'Este. The theme was "Intelligence on the World: Europe and Italy."

Kathleen was asked to give four talks, and she seemed to thoroughly enjoy her role of speaker. She was really like the girl next door. Born in 1951, Kathleen ran unsuccessfully for governor of Maryland in 2002. I would have voted for her! She is a pleasure to be with, so refreshing. Her manners are impeccable, and everybody enjoyed her talks.

She arrived with a friend, Daphna Edwards Ziman, founder of Children Uniting Nations. She is particularly dedicated to children, and in her work, she has branched out to prevent child abuse and neglect. In 1999 Daphna accompanied a delegation on a humanitarian mission to help Kosovo refugees.

One of my dearest friends and an early visitor to the Villa d'Este is another promoter of international unity. The United Nations International School was founded in 1947 by a group of United Nations parents. It started out as a nursery school with twenty very young students of fifteen nationalities, but it soon developed into something much more. In 1961 the school enrolled students from kindergarten to twelfth grade. Sylvia Fuhrman, special representative of the secretary-general for the United Nations International School (and my dear friend), was given the very difficult task of finding a permanent location.

When it was established, the campus was called the Manhattan Campus, designed by Harrison and Abramowitz and built in 1973 with a grant from the Ford Foundation and the Rockefeller Brothers Fund. The City of New York gave them a lease on the property for ninety-nine years at a dollar a year, paid in advance.

But I think one of my favorite visitors of all time was Joseph Heller. We met only ten years before he died in 1999, but when Heller heard that I had worked at the American Red Cross, dishing out coffee and doughnuts to the Fifth Army when Rome was liberated, we decided that was where we met. We repeated it to everybody and we got to believe it. Joseph Heller and his wife, Valerie Humphries, came often to Villa d'Este.

I was so delighted to meet them, thanks to mutual friends. Of course, I had read his masterpiece, *Catch-22*, but I must confess that I'm not quite sure I understand its meaning. The best definition I found is that the title signifies "a no-win situation," and it has entered the English language as common parlance. I hear that the book is studied in U.S. high schools.

When we met, I was in the midst of writing *Villa d'Este Style*, and with the help of Valerie, I convinced Joe to write the foreword for my book. I was so grateful; I will always treasure those last words he wrote for me.

I had not expected ever to write the introductory text for a book devoted to the history and elegance of a luxurious resort hotel, as this book is about the Villa d'Este, outside the Italian village of Cernobbio on Lake Como. But my friendship with Jean Salvadore is strong, my relationship with the management cordial, and the accommodations always thoroughly fulfilling, and it seemed an easier choice, when invited, to comply than to cope with guilty feelings of regret at the appearance of a lack of gratitude and a lack of affection for the people and the place toward which I feel so much. And the book, as you can see by opening it now to just about any page, like the splendid establishment it describes, is easy to praise.

My acquaintance with Jean Salvadore goes back now almost ten years. A widow of Italian descent, she is a woman of a kind one occasionally meets, usually European, with an adventurous past, whose effect upon others she with modesty underestimates.

Though we have known each other for less than a decade, it is highly possible that our paths crossed in Rome more than once over fifty years ago, when I, as a twenty-one-year-old boy in the American Air Corps, came there several times on recreation leave, and she, as a young teenage girl born in Paris of Italian parents and living in Rome, secured employment serving coffee and doughnuts to Americans at the large Red Cross facility in efficient operation there soon after the Germans withdrew from the open city and the advancing Allied forces moved in. The Red Cross building for officers was down near the bottom of the Via Veneto at the Piazza Barberini, and it served as the advantageous assembling point for those of us from the same squadron there at the same time who wished for a breakfast, lunch, or snack of familiar food at prices we could easily afford before taking off for our roamings about the incredible and exciting city of Rome. The memories of the time held by Jean are different from mine, and our experiences of course differ, too. For me and other servicemen there on leave, it was a peaceful place of opulent multiple pleasure; for Jean and her family, existing under the successive occupations of the Germans and the Allies, it was a time of uncertainty and hardship, with indelible memories of fear, cold, curfews, poverty, civic violence between opposing civilian political factions, shortages of food, and long lines for water—water not just for washing but for drinking too."

I have made some extraordinary friends and received some incredible missives from friends and acquaintances alike over the years . . . but I treasure most these personal expressions of contact. Because that's what my life has been all about: the ability to communicate and have contact with literally thousands of people, each of whom has brought something special to my experience and knowledge, and made mine a life worth living and, I hope, worth reporting. If you are still with me, you must come and visit my paradise on earth.

Afterword

Some thirty-nine years ago, Aldo Cicoletti, a retired Milanese financier, decided to move back to Milan so that the Salvadores could move into the "hole in the wall" of the great Villa d'Este mosaic, which became our home. Our house is actually part of the mosaic, but it is invisible to most visitors, because it is covered with ivy and vines and overwhelmed by the drama of the famed mosaic, a national monument of Italy, dating back to the sixteenth century.

When Cicoletti visited twenty-three years later, he looked around, pointed to the tree in front of the entrance, and exclaimed, "I don't remember this tree opposite the entrance."

"That is Luca's tree," I said. "I'll tell you a story.

"Luca and I enjoyed Christmas at Villa d'Este because there was no one around—the hotel is closed. The two of us would go through stacks of books. We would eat when and if we felt like it and sleep whenever we wanted. We would walk in the Villa d'Este park; this was our idea of a holiday.

"One Christmas, we were at home with a nice warm glow coming from the fireplace, and we had never felt more relaxed or happier. Then, suddenly, the doorbell rang. We both jumped up. Who could it be?

"None other than our son, Andrea, who wanted to surprise us for the holiday. Unfortunately, the surprise was on him. My Christmas Eve tradition was that I would have a tree that I had decorated with glass objects that had belonged to my parents, along with all the trimmings. But this year my kids were off on their own; so there was no reason to knock ourselves out.

"My Andrea was indignant: no Christmas tree, no turkey?! Andrea was and is still very sentimental, and he was shocked to find that we had entirely ignored the usual festivities.

"Luca rushed out to buy a tree and returned with one about twenty inches tall, saying that it had roots and I should plant it. This event took place more than twenty years ago, just before Luca died, and today that little tree is taller than the house—about forty feet tall—and stands well higher than the mosaic.

"I am sure that from up above, Luca is watching over his tree."

With this Cicoletti departed, now knowing that his house had been put into good hands.

Some friends selected *The Lady Who Lives in the Wall* as a catchy title for this book of my memories. I had set aside about a dozen titles that did not need to be explained. I thought that *The Lady Who Lives in the Wall* was more intriguing. One of the great secrets of Villa d'Este is that I live in the "hole in the wall." An explanation is in order.

About twelve years ago a gentleman from New York by the name of Tom Goodman spent a week with his family, fifteen in all, at Villa d'Este. We got to know each other, and T.G. confessed that his young son, who would see me going in and out of a little wooden door in the mosaic, was watching me. I soon became known as "the lady who lives in the wall."

Apparently the nickname stuck, because a few years ago I was walking down Park Avenue when suddenly I heard someone calling out, "The lady who lives in the wall!"

Usually New Yorkers would not dream of turning around to see what was going on, but Tom Goodman put on such a show that many people stopped to watch the scene. There were lots of hugs, kisses, and laughter.

This is when I decided that no matter what the title of my book, I would always consider myself "the lady who lives in the wall."

Jean Govoni Salvadore

Chronology

1924 Parents Giancarlo Govoni and Isabella Chiesi marry in Milan

May 16, 1926 Jean Govoni Salvadore born in Paris

1929 Govoni family moves to London and twin brothers Mario and Italo are born

June 11, 1930 Jean's twin brothers Mario and Italo are born

1930 – 1935 Govoni family travels back and forth between London and Paris

1935 Sanctions on Italy force Govonis to move the Venice Lido in Italy; Jean attends school in Switzerland

1936 Sanctions are lifted and Govoni family moves back to Paris and Jean attends French school, then a new Italian school

September 1, 1939 Hitler marches on Poland and WWII begins

1939 Family leaves Paris for Rome with outbreak of WWII; Jean joins Young Italians on Horseback

1941 Jean attends the Classical Lyceum

August 1942 Jean goes on a month's tour of Germany for outstanding German language ability

1942 First air raid alarms in Rome

October 1943 – April 1945 Germans take over Villa d'Este

August 17, 1943 Allies land in Sicily

September 10, 1943 Persichetti instigates Romans to
fight the occupation

October 16, 1943 Jews rounded up from the Roman ghetto

March 24, 1944 Fosse Ardeatine massacre

January 22, 1944 Battle of Anzio

June 4, 1944 Rome liberated; Jean gets behind doughnut
stand at the behest of Stan Anderson (The Donut Man) of the
American Red Cross

June 5, 1944 Celebrations in Rome

June 10, 1944 Jean appears in US newspapers (International
News, Associated Press, and UPI) as the first Roman to work for
the American Red Cross

April 1945 Americans liberate Northern Italy

May 5, 1945 War ends in Europe

1946 Jeans works at the American Red Cross (Rest Center) at
Hotel Bernini in Rome

March 1, 1947 Jean goes to TWA office in Rome hoping to become
flight hostess but she is turned down because she does not have an
American passport

1948 Jean is appointed as the full-time public relations
representative for TWA

September 15, 1948 During a black tie gala and fashion show
Pia Bellentani murders her lover, Carlo Sacchi, in Villa d'Este nightclub

April 30, 1949 Jean and Luca Salvadore marry

1950 Holy Year

1952 Jean's son Andrea born

1955 Jean's daughter Claudia born

1960 The term "paparazzi" originates from Federico Fellini's film *La Dolce Vita*

August 25, 1960 Summer Olympics held in Rome

1961 Jean becomes a columnist for the Italian magazine *Amica*, a weekly insert to the *Corriere della Sera* newspaper

1962 Jean and Luca buy a villa in the seaside resort town of Fregene, Italy

1963 Luca leaves TWA to become the head of sales for the new Hilton Hotel, located on Monte Mario in Rome

June 3, 1963 Pope John XXIII dies

June 21, 1963 Cardinal Giovanni Battista Montini succeeds as Pope

1964 Jean's daughter Claudia's first Holy Communion

1966 Jean and family move to Milan when Luca accepts public relations director job for Angelo Rizzoli; Jean leaves her job at TWA

October 1967 Jean begins at Villa d'Este; Villa d'Este Cooking School begins

1971 Villa d'Este hosts Christie's of London auction

1973 Villa d'Este Centennial

1981 *Cooking Ideas from Villa d'Este* by Jean Govoni
Salvadore published

1988 Viva Hollywood at Villa d'Este

January 22, 1988 Luca passes away

April 1999 *Villa d'Este Cookbook* by Jean Govoni Salvadore
published by Stewart, Tabori & Chang

June 2000 *Villa d'Este Style* by Jean Govoni Salvadore published
by Rizzoli International Publications

October 2006 *Tales of Risotto* by Jean Govoni Salvadore and
Luciano Parolari published by Glitterati

April 2011 *My Dolce Vita* by Jean Govoni Salvadore is published
by Glitterati

Acknowledgments

It is impossible to express my gratitude for all the assistance I received in assembling my memoirs, but I will do my best. I think I should start by thanking my son Andrea and daughter Claudia, along, with their families, who will enjoy reading about their Grannie, I hope.

Next I want to thank my dear friend and colleague, Pamela Fiori, for all the years of friendship and, in particular, for the lovely Foreword she has contributed to this book.

I also want to thank my publisher, Marta Hallett, who is also my friend; and who was introduced to me by Larry Ashmead, the legendary HarperCollins editor, who died while I was in the throes of writing these thank-yous. He was a formidable person and friend.

My manuscript was handwritten (pencil and eraser), although I must confess that I did try to use a computer, but it didn't work. As my son Andrea would say: " Mother, sorry but you are not hi-tech minded. Keep using your pencil and let the words flow." Maybe I will turn to a computer for my next book, before my ninetieth birthday.

And, as always, my gratitude goes to Annamaria Duvia, who has assisted me from my earliest years at Villa d'Este. She and Luciano Parolari started working at Villa d'Este in 1967, as I did. Forty-three years together and in the same place is quite a record.

I never would have completed the book without the assistance of the "family" that I have acquired these years at Villa d'Este, beginning with Jean-Marc Droulers, President and CEO of the hotel. And then there are the more than three hundred employees of the hotel, many of whom have been on the job for forty years, who are still not ready to retire, like me.

I wish I could mention all the friends who have helped me through these last 64 years. Following is a very reduced list of hotel guest with whom I try to keep in touch.

Julie Amsterdam
Alix and Richard Barthelmes
Mary Ellen Barton
Lucy Zahran and Jim Bonorris
Anne and Nael Bunni
Karon Cullen and Rick Meyer III
Avril and Ian Dewar
Anita and Paul De Domenico
Edward De Luca
Francine and Halbert Drexler
Bill Fischer
Sylvia Howard Fuhrman
Harry Hinson
Beth and Skip Keesal
Janet and Ed Kelly
Julie and Michael Lacher
Eve and Bill Lilley
Trudy Mannheimer and Hugh Feehan
Karen Kriendler Nelson
Sandy and Ron Olin
Irene Pollin and family
Gene Silbert
Barbara and Manfred Stalla
Shelley and David Stevens
Jane Taylor
Hope Warner
Valerie Ann Wilson
Bill Wright and Barry Raine

Mildred Amico
Maria Battaglia
Alexandra Mayes Birnbaum
Kimberley and David Brody
Barbara Cameron
Harriet Delsener
Sheila Daniels
Lenny and Chas De Fanti
Anita Draycott
Ida and Perry Fishbein
Leda and Jack Frazee
Elizabeth and Bob Harmon
Elizabeth and Michael Jacobs
John Kiley
Kathleen and Fred Krehbiel
Roslyn and Ted Leopold
Molly and James McIlvenny
Sissie and Billy Morris III
Nancy Novogrod
Alice Gesar Papazian
Sheila Schott
Dawn Smith
Rudi Steele and John Cargile
Ellen Sweeney
Veronica and Stuart Timperley
Nina and Jens Werner
Wayne Winnick
Yolanda Wright

And here are some of my friends from "downunder:"

Sir Ron Brierley

Joy Dodds

Helms and Samantha Slaney

Robin Henderson

Patricia Holden

Bruce Jarrett

Noelene Keen Ward

Barbara and Bernie Leser

Lynden Milan

Maggie Oehlbeck

Elizabeth Rich

The Rossi Family

Beverley Sutherland Smith

Warwick Vyner

June Dally-Watkins

Godchildren Danielle Rossi

Judith Forbes

Christine Hogan

Maggie Hughes

Kate and Reg Johnstone

Regina King

Carolyn Lockhart

Lynne Mullins

Grant Pearce

Richard Roberts

Leo Schofield

Michael Visontay

Leslie Walford

Jean Govoni Salvadore

Citations and Photography Credits

Quotations

PAGE 9: From *The Autobiography of Mark Twain* by Mark Twain and edited by Charles Neider, New York: Harper Perennial Modern Classics, 2000.

PAGE 18: From *A Postillion Struck by Lightning* by Dirk Bogarde, San Francisco: Phoenix Books, 2005; and Page 19, An Orderly Man by Dirk Bogarde, London: Penguin Books, 1992.

PAGE 84: From *I Sette Peccati di Hollywood (The Seven Sins of Hollywood)* by Oriana Fallacci, Milan: Longansi/Rizzoli, date 1958.

PAGE 99: From *Edith Wharton's Gardens* by Vivian Russell, London: Frances Lincoln, 1997; and Page 149: "Grand Hotel Villa d'Este," by David Leavitt, from Travel & Leisure magazine, October 7, 1997.

Images

The author would like to thank the copyright holders, listed below, who have generously contributed the artwork that illustrates this book:

PHOTO SECTION ONE: Irving Hoffman: page 32.

PHOTO SECTION TWO: Aeronews: pages 31, 39; International News Photos: pages 5, 6, 30 (top); Photoreporter: pages 4, 8; C.B. Poletto: page 37; Publiphoto: pages 7, 16-18 (top), 19-28, 32, 35, 40; United Press Photos: page 18 (bottom).

PHOTO SECTION THREE: *Corriera della Serra:* page 11; Everett Collection: page 10; Ottica Piffaretti: pages 5, 6, 24-26, 28-30; Elizabeth Rich: page 16; Johnny Rozsa: page 22; *The Sun:* page 14; Archivio Fotografico Vasconi: pages 7, 20, 26.

PHOTO SECTION FOUR: Carlo Cerchioli: pages 6-7; Ottica Piffaretti: pages 2-3, 16-17, 22-25; Vasconi: pages 4 (top), 28-29

Any photographs not credited come from the personal collection of the author. Every effort has been made to locate all copyright holders of artwork in this book and if any have been overlooked or are inaccurately credited, please contact the publisher for correction.

Index